A Biblical Search for the Church Christ Founded

A Biblical Search for the Church Christ Founded

Foreword by H. E. Cardinal Francis Arinze

Linus F. Clovis

GRACEWING

First published in England in 2012
by
Gracewing
2 Southern Avenue
Leominster
Herefordshire HR6 0QF
United Kingdom
www.gracewing.co.uk

Nihil obstat: ✠Most Rev Gabriel Malzaire, Bishop of Roseau, *Censor Librorum*
Imprimatur: ✠Most Rev Robert Rivas, OP, Archbishop of Castries
Date: 19 September 2011

The *Nihil obstat* and *Imprimatur* are official declarations that a book or
pamphlet is free of doctrinal or moral error. No implication is contained
therein that those who have granted *Nihil obstat* and *Imprimatur* agree
with the contents, opinions or statements expressed.

ISBN 978 085244 771 0

On the cover: Mosaic of Christ the Good Shepherd, from the
mausoleum of Galla Placidia, Ravenna, c. 425-426.

Typeset by Gracewing

Printed and bound by Shore Books and Design, King's Lynn, Norfolk

CONTENTS

Dedication

With filial devotion to Mary Immaculate,
and in union with my brothers
Christopher, Gregory, Joseph and Henry–Andre,
I offer this work to the most blessed and glorious Trinity
in gratitude for the gift of our parents,
Henry and Audrey,
who transmitted to us the gift of life,
both natural and supernatural.

Foreword

Father Linus F. Clovis has written a good book. He has examined with considerable competence and dedication the most important question of the founding of the Church by our beloved Lord and Saviour, Jesus Christ. He has marshalled abundant Scriptural texts to help any unbiased person identify the one, true, holy and apostolic Church which Jesus founded. Demonstrating great acquaintance with the Holy Scriptures, and with occasional quotations from the early Church Fathers, he has shown clearly that the Roman Catholic Church is the Church that Jesus founded. Thank you, Father Clovis. And may all who read this work draw the inevitable conclusion.

✠ Francis Cardinal Arinze

Cardinal-Bishop of Velletri-Segni

Prefect Emeritus of the Congregation for Divine Worship and the Discipline of the Sacraments

Preface

I hope that the reader of this text, *A Biblical Search for the Church Christ Founded*, will find it both informative and useful. Excluding the Scripture quotations, it has evolved from a twelve–page document that I had prepared as a teaching guide for the catechists of the Parish of the Purification of the Blessed Virgin Mary, Laborie, St Lucia.

On being appointed parish priest of Laborie, in September 2007, my first concern was for the spiritual life of the children enrolled in the First Communion and Confirmation catechetical programmes. I believe, and I am fully convinced, that the catechetical formation children receive impacts greatly on the manner in which they live their Christian commitment.

I learned from the catechists that the majority of our children, upon Confirmation, exit the Church, either through cessation of practice or by joining one of the many sects in St Lucia that actively recruit them. As a first step to remedy this haemorrhaging of the Church in St Lucia, I put together a little booklet to give an outline of the answer to the pressing question *Where is the Church Christ founded?* The catechists' positive response to the booklet was encouraging, especially when they asked that I develop it more fully.

In developing the teaching guide, I had to keep in mind the many misinterpretations of Scripture with which our children are bombarded, confused and seduced. It was, therefore, necessary not only to show our children that the *Church Christ founded* is clearly identifiable from Scripture but also, to equip them with the means to recognise her from among the numerous claimants. Additionally, I thought it should be a useful guide for those people of goodwill who are searching for the *Church Christ founded* but do not have the skill or the time to sift through the various claims.

In His great high priestly prayer on the night He was betrayed, Christ prayed *'ut unum sint'* (Jn 17:21). Present–day Christians are not responsible for Christian disunity. We are, however, heirs of the sad dissent generated in previous centuries. Therefore, in these days of ecumenism, it is right that we should seek Christian unity since Christ prayed for the unity of His followers. Though this transcends human powers and gifts, nonetheless, with our hope 'in the prayer of Christ for the Church, in the love of the Father for us, and in the power of the Holy Spirit' the road to achieving unity is made easier by the saving truth that enlightens the intellect and fortifies the will. That is, forging doctrine out of contradictory opinions will not lead to unity but unity will come from the saving truth spoken in charity (Ep 4:15).

Acknowledgements

This was my first attempt at writing anything that resembles a book and there were many times when I thought I would never complete it. The time span between the original booklet and the completion of this book was about one year. Over that period, several people were instrumental for ensuring the realisation of this book. To those people I shall always be indebted.

I would like, however, to pay special recognition to my mother, Audrey, my brother, Greg and his wife Aghi who supported and encouraged me every step of the way. The enthusiasm of Colleen Bayer of Family Life International, New Zealand, was the driving force that spurred me towards the end. My gratitude also goes out both to my brother, Chris and Daphne MacLeod for their input and suggestions after they had read the first version and to Robert Haddad and Loyola Devaux for their critical reading of the finished draft. Additionally, I must extend singular acknowledgement to His Eminence, Francis Cardinal Arinze for his kindness in reading the manuscript, for his gentleness at correction and especially for his gracious endorsement contained in the Foreword. My greatest thanks, however, is owed to Geraldine Samuel (Gene), a teacher at St Joseph's Convent, who journeyed tirelessly devoting countless hours to analysing, proofreading, editing and correcting. Gene's invaluable contribution, mingled with humour and fun was able to lighten up many a dreary moment and has made writing quite an enjoyable experience. A note of thanks is also owed to my nephew Daniel for his patience and for the many hours of computer assistance given. To everyone who supported me in this work, a heartfelt 'Thank You'.

Note to Reader

This text was originally conceived as a teaching aid and this is still its overall purpose; hence, the format adopted.

Each chapter contains a Preamble, which gives an overall view of the subject matter. The Exposition follows the Preamble and develops the chapter, where appropriate, with relevant Scripture quotations. The Catholic Edition of the Revised Standard Version of the Bible is used throughout this text. Each chapter ends with some Points to Remember, which identify the key points of the chapter.

The Conclusion is drawn from the preceding chapters and the Epilogue attempts to answer some queries or objections that may arise concerning the Church Christ founded.

Illustrations

Illustrations from *Die Bibel in Bildern* by Julius Schnorr von Carolsfeld (1794–1872): Figures 1, 2, 4, 5, 14, 23.

Illustrations from H. D. Northrop, *Treasures of the Bible* (International Publishing Company, 1894): Figures 3, 7, 9, 10, 11, 12, 13, 15, 16, 17, 18, 19, 20, 21, 22.

Woodcut from old Missal: Figure 6.

Matthaeus Merian the Elder (1593–1650): Figure 8.

1

Introduction

Preamble

All civilisations have a religious dimension that recognises the existence of unseen spiritual realities. In order to commune with these spiritual realities, various types of religion have emerged and fall into only one of two possible categories: either they are natural or they are revealed. Natural religion encapsulates all human efforts to reach the divine in order to establish some communion with the spiritual realm. Revealed religion, on the other hand, is characterised by the divine in search of the human, that is, the Creator in pursuit of the creature on whom He wishes to confer some benefit.

The reasoning and mediations of a few diligent and inspired people about spiritual matters have led to the discovery of certain truths about God, which constitute the basis for natural religion. Unfortunately, these discoveries are arrived at over long periods and the truths contained therein are frequently mingled with errors. This can be deduced from the differences and contradictions found amongst the various expressions of natural religion.

Some truths about God are inaccessible to human beings. God has chosen to reveal these truths, some of which have been committed to writing; these truths constitute the basis for revealed religion. Revealed religion, then, is a mosaic of transcendental truths learned through divine revelation, together with natural knowledge, built up by reason that, in its fullness, will be found in the Person of Jesus Christ, the Son of God.

Exposition

The definitive characteristic of human nature is the ability to reason. Reason is the art by which rational beings propose and consider explanations of issues concerning cause and effect, true and false, and what is good or bad. It is closely identified with the ability to self–consciously change beliefs, attitudes, traditions and institutions, and therefore it is associated with the human capacity for freedom and self-determination. In short, human beings use this ability to discover truth, which is nothing other than the conformity of the mind and reality.

Experience, however, shows that the interpretations, and hence the conclusions arrived at, are dependent upon the reasoning process being applied to the information received through the senses. Consequently, insufficient information or faulty reasoning can result in human beings falling into error, being deceived or being misled. For example, if one depends only on what one sees, the earth will appear to be flat, but one can accept that it is somewhat spherical only by accepting the judgment of experts or by seeing it for oneself from outer space. In the search for truth, especially where the senses provide limited relevant information, those with the expertise must sift through the accumulated experiences, discoveries and deductions of the human family.

Now the human mind is able to deduce some things about God, since God has left signs and traces of His existence and nature in the created universe:

> For what can be known about God is plain to them, because God has shown it to them. Ever since the creation of the world his invisible nature, namely, his eternal power and deity, has been clearly perceived in the things that have been made (Rm 1:19–20).

Figure 1: *God creates light*

Human perversity, however, often leads to a misreading of the signs relating to God's invisible nature, to the suppression of truth (Rm 1:18), to the rejection of it (Rm 1:25) and eventually to the acceptance and embracing of error. (Jn 5:43) Christ who worked many signs to validate the truth of what He said, complained, '*I have come in my Father's name, and you do not receive me; if another comes in his own name, him you will receive*' (Jn 5:43). It can be said more generally that although the perverse

> knew God they did not honour him as God or give thanks to him, but they became futile in their thinking and their senseless minds were darkened. Claiming to be wise, they became fools, and exchanged the glory of the immortal God for images resembling mortal man or birds or animals or reptiles (Rm 1:21–23).

Now, it is clearly evident that human reason can deduce some truths about God's nature such as His existence and His goodness. There are, however, other truths such as God's existence as a personal being and the mysteries of His inner life that are quite beyond the grasp of the human intellect: *'For what person knows a man's thoughts except the spirit of the man which is in him? So also no one comprehends the thoughts of God except the Spirit of God'* (1Co 2:11).

If these humanly inaccessible truths about God's nature are necessary for human salvation, then, it belongs to God's goodness to reveal them since *'without faith it is impossible to please him. For whoever would draw near to God must believe that he exists and that he rewards those who seek him'* (Heb 11:6). Further, it is plainly evident to human reason that truth is an essential quality for establishing and maintaining any meaningful relationship. Therefore, God, however He is perceived, must be truthful in His self–disclosure if there is to be any meaningful relationship with Him. Additionally, since human knowledge and understanding develop with time, God, like a good teacher, does not reveal everything about Himself at once, but in stages as He walks with His children through all the vicissitudes of human history.

The interaction of the human and the divine gives rise to certain responses exhibited in attitudes and behaviours. The sum total of these is called religion, that is, the things to be believed, to be hoped for and to be loved.

Natural religion

The human capacity for self–reflection and transcendence has, throughout history and in all civilisations, given rise to a search for the divine and, consequently, has produced or established various branches of natural religion. As Plutarch, the first century Greek historian, noted, *'You will find cities without walls, without literature, and without the arts and sciences of civilised life, but you will never find a city without priests and altars, or which does not have sacrifices offered to the gods.'*

While natural religions may contain some spiritual truths, such as God's existence or man's fallen nature, they also embrace erroneous principles that lead to, among other beliefs and practices, pantheism, polytheism and idolatry.

For all men who were ignorant of God were foolish by nature;
and they were unable from the good things
that are seen to know him who exists,
nor did they recognise the craftsman
while paying heed to his works;
but they supposed that either fire or wind or swift air,
or the circle of the stars, or turbulent water,
of the luminaries of heaven were the gods that rule the world.
If through delight in the beauty of these things
men assumed them to be gods,
let them know how much better than these is their Lord,
for the author of beauty created them.
And if men were amazed at their power and working,
let them perceive from them how much more
powerful is he who formed them.
For from the greatness and beauty of created things
comes a corresponding perception of their Creator.
Yet these men are little to be blamed,
for perhaps they go astray while seeking God
and desiring to find him.
For as they live among his works
they keep searching, and they trust in what they see,
because the things that are seen are beautiful.
Yet again, not even they are to be excused;
for if they had the power to know so much that
they could investigate the world,
how did they fail to find sooner the Lord of these things?
But miserable, with their hopes set on dead things,
are the men who give the name 'gods'
to the works of men's hands,
gold and silver fashioned with skill,
and likenesses of animals, or a useless stone,
the work of an ancient hand (Ws 13:1–10).

The Greeks, for instance, were not only believers in the existence of many gods but, they were also scrupulous in worshipping them to the extent that they worshipped even the gods they did not know, as St Paul observed:

> Paul, standing in the middle of the Areopagus, said: 'Men of Athens, I perceive that in every way you are very religious. For as I passed along, and observed the objects of your worship, I found also an altar with this inscription, 'To an unknown god'. What therefore you worship as unknown, this I proclaim to you' (Ac 17:22–23).

From the Athenian approach to religion, it is evident that all branches of natural religion are equivalent and that, perhaps, like political systems, are beneficial only for a particular time, in a particular place and for a particular people.

Revealed religion

Corresponding to the human search for the divine, as is expressed in all branches of natural religion, there is the divine search for the human, which is found only in Judaism and its fulfilment, Christianity. There can only be one revealed religion '*For God is not a God of confusion but of peace*' (1Co 14:33). If there were another revealed religion then, to distinguish between the two, there would need to be some difference or contradiction between them, which would imply that God was not being truthful in His self–disclosure and, consequently, He would be creating confusion. This, in turn, would not only cast doubt on His wisdom, authority and goodness but would also destroy any possibility of a meaningful relationship with Him. In short, He would not be '*a God of faithfulness and without iniquity,* (who is) *just and right* (and whose) *ways are justice*' (Dt 32:4). Judaism and Christianity, however, together form one divine revelation and authenticate each other in as much as Christianity fulfils the Jewish prophecies. Thus, the New Testament fulfils and confirms the Old, while the Old Testament predicts and prefigures the New (Mt 26:56; Lk 24:44; Ac 3:18; Rm 1:2; Rev 10:7). God's self–disclosure, then, is found uniquely in the Judeo–Christian dispensation:

He declares his word to Jacob,
his statutes and ordinances to Israel.
He has not dealt thus with any other nation;
they do not know his ordinances (Ps 147:19–20).

The Judeo–Christian revelation is a historical religion that has chronicled God's self–disclosure and His intervention in human affairs in a number of holy books, collectively called the Bible. The first Book of the Bible, Genesis records the story of the Creator's initial search for His human creatures, Adam and Eve, who, because of their disobedience, hid themselves from Him.

> And they heard the sound of the Lord God walking in the garden in the cool of the day, and the man and his wife hid themselves from the presence of the Lord God among the trees of the garden. But the Lord God called to the man, and said to him, 'Where are you?' And he said, 'I heard the sound of thee in the garden, and I was afraid, because I was naked; and I hid myself' (Gn 3:8–10).

The Bible also chronicles specific divine interventions in history, which were landmarks in God's search for His human creatures.

First, He chose Abram through whom He would establish a family and nation:

> The Lord said to Abram, 'Go from your country and your kindred and your father's house to the land that I will show you. And I will make of you a great nation …'
> So Abram went, as the Lord had told him… (Gn 12:1–4).

Second, He called Moses to lead the descendents of Abram, whose name God had changed to Abraham (Gn 17:5), out of Egypt where they had been enslaved, to a land where they would become His people:

God called … out of the bush, 'Moses, Moses!' And he said, 'Here am I' … He said, 'I am the God of your father, the God of Abraham, the God of Isaac, and the God of Jacob … I have seen the affliction of my people who are in Egypt, and have heard their cry because of their taskmasters; I know their sufferings, and I have come down to deliver them out of the hand of the Egyptians, and to bring them up out of that land to a good and broad land, a land flowing with milk and honey, to the place of the Canaanites, the Hittites, the Amorites, the Perizzites, the Hivites, and the Jebusites … Come, I will send you to Pharaoh that you may bring forth my people, the sons of Israel, out of Egypt' (Ex 3:4–11).

Third, God constituted His people, the children of Israel, as a nation when He chose David to be king over them. He then added a promise that one of David's descendents would establish a kingdom that would last forever:

Thus says the Lord of hosts, I took you … from following the sheep, that you should be prince over my people Israel; and I have been with you wherever you went, and have cut off all your enemies from before you; and I will make for you a great name, like the name of the great ones of the earth. And I will appoint a place for my people Israel, and will plant them, that they may dwell in their own place, and be disturbed no more; and violent men shall afflict them no more, as formerly, from the time that I appointed judges over my people Israel; and I will give you rest from all your enemies … I will raise up your offspring after you, …, and I will establish his kingdom. … your house and your kingdom shall be made sure for ever before me; your throne shall be established for ever (2S 7:8–16).

The divine self–disclosure to the Jewish people was made through the prophets of Israel and is recorded in the Old Testament. This self-disclosure includes revealing God's plan in regard to Israel. That is, He would choose of a family (Abraham), a people (Moses), and a nation (David), in which, at the appropriate time, He would manifest Himself. The public completion of this self-disclosure occurred on the Mount of the Transfiguration when, God, revealed by Christ as Father, spoke, fully and directly, for the last time, saying, *'This is my beloved Son, with whom I am well pleased; listen to him'* (Mt 17:5). To hear the Son is to hear the Father who sent Him (Lk 10:16). Thus, the fullness of divine self-disclosure is to be found in Christ, the Son of God, as the Evangelist testifies *'we have seen and testify that the Father has sent his Son as the Saviour of the world'* (1Jn 4:14) and as the letter to the Hebrews makes clear:

> In many and various ways God spoke of old to our fathers by the prophets, but in these last days he has spoken to us by a Son, whom he appointed the heir of all things, through whom also he created the world (Heb 1:1–2).

Christ's revelation is the completion of the divine self–disclosure for *'when the time had fully come, God sent forth his Son, born of woman, born under the law, to redeem those who were under the law'* (Ga 4:4–5). This revelation is recorded in the New Testament, which is an account of the life and mission of Jesus Christ, the Word who is God (Jn 1:1), who *'became flesh and dwelt among us'* (Jn 1:14). It is the story of God in search of His human creatures, of God who *'so loved the world that he gave his only Son, that whoever believes in him should not perish but have eternal life'* (Jn 3:16). Eternal life is offered to the whole human race but, since Christ's life on earth spanned a brief thirty three years, it was necessary that there be some means by which the offer of eternal life would remain accessible to future generations. Christ Himself ensured this accessibility by choosing certain representatives to speak unerringly in His name so that the essential message He delivered would retain its divine authority and remain the same for all time and for all peoples:

> All this is from God, who through Christ reconciled us to himself and gave us the ministry of reconciliation; that is, in Christ, God was reconciling the world

to himself, not counting their trespasses against them, and entrusting to us the message of reconciliation. So we are ambassadors for Christ, God making his appeal through us. We beseech you on behalf of Christ, be reconciled to God (2Co 5:18–20).

Points to Remember

a. *Religious belief is found among all peoples, in every society and in all civilisations, and is either natural or revealed.*

b. *All natural religions are human efforts to communicate with God.*

c. *Revealed religion is God's self–disclosure and direct intervention in human history.*

d. *Judaism and its fulfilment, Christianity, form one complete divine self–disclosure.*

e. *The Judaic and Christian revelations are recorded in the Old and New Testaments respectively.*

f. *The central message of Judaism is God's choice of Abram and his descendants to form a family, people and nation into which His only–begotten Son, at the fullness of time, would be born.*

g. *The central message of Christianity is that the promises God made to Abram and his descendants are fulfilled in the Person of Our Lord Jesus Christ.*

h. *Christ offers eternal life to the whole human race and, to ensure that His message and offer would remain the same and valid for all time and for all peoples, He chose and authorised certain representatives to speak in His name throughout the ages.*

2

The Christian landscape

Preamble

Christianity is a revealed religion founded by Jesus Christ whose coming was prophesied in the Old Testament. Breaking from the mould of its Jewish origins, Christianity expanded rapidly in the Roman Empire once Gentiles were embraced as followers of Christ. From its beginning, the Christian religion was constituted as a definite social entity, called the Church. As the centuries progressed, various philosophical, political and religious disagreements occurred among some members who, unable to accept the ecclesial authority established by Christ, set up their own church communities. The most significant and lasting ruptures were those of AD 1054, which resulted in the formation of the Orthodox Churches and those of the sixteenth century, which gave rise to the Protestant communities. Today, there are over thirty-eight thousand such denominations, each differing from the others, each calling itself Christian and each one claiming to be the true Church or a part of the true Church. This multitude of denominations can be divided into three basic groups: the Catholic Church, the Eastern Churches, and the Protestant Communities.

Exposition

Most Jews still await the appearance of the Messiah whose coming is predicted in the Old Testament. Christians, however, believe that *'when the time had fully come, God sent forth his Son, born of woman, born under the law, to redeem those who were under the law'* (Ga 4:4–5). They believe that Jesus Christ is that Son and the promised Messiah and that, in His person and in the events of His life, He fulfilled all the Old Testament prophecies concerning the Messiah. Christ is undoubtedly a concrete historical person who, in AD 33, *'was crucified under Pontius Pilate, died, was buried and rose from the dead'*. Initially, His followers were Jews. From among these He chose twelve men whom He called apostles.

Figure 2: *Christ sends out the twelve Apostles*

The Apostles were to be primarily the eyewitnesses to His life, death and Resurrection and secondarily they would vouch for the actual content of His teaching and the reality of His miracles (Lk 1:2). These twelve Apostles formed the nucleus of the early Church, with Simon Peter, specifically chosen by Christ Himself, as its first Leader. From AD 33 until the death of the last Apostle, St John the Evangelist in AD 100, when public divine revelation officially ceased, the early Church enjoyed the physical presence of the Apostles and so it is referred to as the Apostolic Church. Within a few years of its founding, the nascent Church experienced not only a rapid numerical growth but also, a phenomenal geographic expansion. The former was because of the admission of Gentiles, that is, those who were not Jews into full Church membership. The latter was the result of Church missionary activity in non-Jewish territories.

Christianity spread rapidly throughout the Roman Empire and Church communities were organised in various cities and territories around leaders called bishops, who exercised spiritual authority over a definite geographical area called a diocese. When theological disputes arose, they were resolved authoritatively and definitively by General Councils of bishops under the presiding authority of the Bishop of Rome.

Prior to the Fifth Century, the Christian world was nothing other than the one Catholic Church with branches, each using its own cultural genius, language and liturgical form to manifest the essential unity of doctrine, sacraments and hierarchical authority.

In 431, however, the Council of Ephesus condemned Nestorianism, the theological opinion of Nestorius, Bishop of Constantinople, which held that there were two distinct persons in Christ and that, consequently, Mary could not be the Mother of God. The Church in Persia, by embracing this opinion, became Nestorian and, because of its vigorous missionary spirit, established daughter churches holding Nestorian beliefs in central Asia and as far as Mongolia and China.

Twenty years later in 451, the Council of Chalcedon condemned another theological opinion called Mono-physitism. This opinion, proposed by Eutyches, held that there was in Christ one nature—the divine that would absorb the human nature in itself. This belief was accepted by the Church in West Syria, by most of the Church of Alexandria (i.e. North Africa and later, Ethiopia), by Armenia and, in the sixteenth century, by a portion of the St Thomas Christians in India.

The Churches of Constantinople and Rome remained faithful to the teachings of the General Councils of Ephesus and Chalcedon and, hence, called themselves 'Orthodox' meaning, Churches that hold the true and correct teaching of the early Christian Church, as promulgated by these two Councils. The Nestorian and Monophysite Churches, on the other hand, are designated the Ancient Churches of the East.

Thus, at the end of the first millennium there was one worldwide Church called the Catholic Church, adhering to the definitive decisions of the General Councils and governed by the bishops of the eastern and western dioceses of the old Roman Empire under the spiritual headship of the Bishop of Rome, the successor to Simon Peter.

In AD 1054, the eastern dioceses, largely for political reasons, separated from Rome to become the Orthodox Churches. They were, and still are, divided along political, national, cultural and linguistic lines and comprise Churches such as the Russian, Greek, Rumanian, Serbian, Antiochean, Bulgarian and Coptic Churches. Although they rejected the supreme spiritual authority of the Bishop of Rome, they have nonetheless preserved the beliefs and practices of the Apostolic Church, especially the Bible, the Tradition, the Sacraments and the Divine Liturgy. The main dispute between the Orthodox Churches and the Catholic Church is one of authority, not the authority of Christ but of the juridical authority conferred by Christ on Peter to govern the Church. Hence, they are referred to as schismatic from the Greek word meaning 'to split'.

The independent and different Protestant communities originate with the break from the Bishop of Rome by Martin Luther (1517), John Calvin (1533) and Henry VIII (1534). Today, there are approximately thirty–eight thousand (38,000) different Protestant communities. While each Protestant community believes and preaches something marginally or, in many cases, even substantially different from the others, each one claims for itself biblical inspiration and purports to be the true Christian Church, as founded by Christ Himself, or an authentic expression or part of it. Protestantism rejects the authority of the Bishop of Rome, the sacramental system understood as the means whereby sanctifying grace is conferred, as well as other doctrines of the Apostolic Church. As such, they are referred to as heretical, from the Greek word meaning 'to choose'. Consequently, because it has no universal governing authority, Protestantism has become a general religious movement where it is possible to select from among the beliefs of primitive Christianity and the authoritative teachings of Church Councils up until the breakaway in the sixteenth century, what should be believed, what should be taught and, since behaviour follows belief, what ought to be done.

The Christian Commonwealth suffered a further rupture with the schism of the Old Catholics. The name 'Old Catholics' refers to the various national churches that at different times separated from the Catholic Church. The initial rupture began with the Church of Utrecht in Holland, which separated from Rome in 1724 over the Jansenism of some of its members, including their archbishop, Petrus Codde. (Jansenism is a theological opinion that claims human freewill is incapable of any moral goodness.) They were subsequently joined by German, Austrian and Swiss Catholics who took issue with the First Vatican Council's definition, in 1870, of papal infallibility and by Polish, Croat and Yugoslav immigrants who had difficulty integrating into the American Anglo–Saxon dominated church. The Declaration of Utrecht in 1889 accepted the first seven General Councils of the Church but rejected, among other things, the primacy of the Bishop of Rome. Consequently, the Old Catholics are in a position similar to that of the Eastern Churches.

In sum, the Catholic and Eastern Churches hold to the doctrine of the Communion of Saints and have a corporate view of the Church as the Body of Christ. Protestantism, on the other hand, asserts an individualistic Christianity that focuses on one's personal relationship with Jesus Christ to the exclusion of any indispensable need for a Church or other visible organisation. However, as it shall be shown, faith in Jesus Christ not only obliges the Christian to have a total trust in and an unquestioning commitment to Him, but also to accept and to practise what He taught, and to belong to and obey, in all matters of faith and morals, the institution He established specifically to continue His work of salvation in the world.

Points to Remember

a. *Christ is the Messiah spoken of in the prophecies of the Old Testament.*

b. *Christianity is a revealed religion founded by Jesus Christ.*

c. *Christ founded a Church with a nucleus of twelve Apostles. Embracing Jews and Gentiles, this Apostolic Church grew rapidly during the first century and spread throughout the Roman Empire.*

d. *The Christian communities in cities and other areas were called churches. These were organised around leaders called bishops, who governed geographical areas called dioceses.*

e. *Initially, Christians were all united in the one Church under the spiritual authority of the Bishop of Rome, the successor of Simon Peter.*

f. *Internal disputes and differences in the interpretation of Holy Scripture and the application of moral teaching to the changing challenges of time, led to breakaway churches being formed, and all claiming to be the authentic Church of Jesus Christ, or part of it.*

g. *The main divisions within Christianity are the Catholic Church, the Eastern and Old Catholic Churches, and the Protestant Communities.*

h. *The Eastern Churches fall into two camps: the Ancient Eastern Churches that are heterodox insofar as they reject the teachings of some General Councils of the Church and the Orthodox Churches which are in partial communion with the Catholic Church.*

i. *The Protestant Communities reject the spiritual authority of the Bishop of Rome as well as some of the teachings and practices of the Apostolic Church, and enjoy a lesser degree of communion with the Catholic Church than the Orthodox Churches.*

j. *The Catholic and Eastern Churches, in general, view the Church of Christ as a visible society, or body of believers, whose members are joined to Christ as well as to each other. Protestantism, on the other hand, asserts an individualistic Christianity that focuses on one's personal relationship with Jesus Christ to the exclusion of any indispensable need for a Church or other visible organisation.*

3

The Church in Prophecy

Preamble

The precise fulfilment of the Old Testament prophecies, which were made over a period covering nearly two thousand years, offers a weighty argument for the supernatural character of the Christian revelation. Consequently, a study of the prophetic utterances regarding the Church would be helpful in establishing the credentials of the Church when it would have appeared. The prophecies of the Old Testament give specific details about the life and work of the Messiah. In particular, they mention His establishment of a kingdom, which would embrace and unite the entire human race. This kingdom, endowed with a new and mystical sacrificial system, would be governed by an authority deriving from the Messiah Himself, would proclaim truths derived from divine revelation and would have a priesthood that sanctifies its members.

Exposition

Since '*the Lord God does nothing, without revealing his secret to his servants the prophets*' (Am 3:7), the prophets of the Old Testament foretold many events that both identify the person and outline the mission of the Messiah. The prophets did not receive these insights into the life and work of the

Messiah for their own benefit but, rather, the prophetic message was given that those who were to receive the Gospel of Christ might have their faith strengthened by it, as St Peter points out in the following passage:

> The prophets who prophesied of the grace that was to be yours searched and inquired about this salvation; they inquired what person or time was indicated by the Spirit of Christ within them when predicting the sufferings of Christ and the subsequent glory. It was revealed to them that they were serving not themselves but you, in the things which have now been announced to you by those who preached the good news to you through the Holy Spirit sent from heaven (1P 1:10–11).

An integral part of the Messiah's mission would be the establishment of a kingdom, whose distinguishing characteristics the prophets of the Old Testament described with great precision. During His ministry, Christ clearly affirmed on several occasions that the prophecies relating to the Messiah and His work were fulfilled in His own person. After His temptation in the wilderness, Christ returned to Nazareth and, going to the Synagogue, read a passage from the Prophet Isaiah. He then declared, *'Today this scripture has been fulfilled in your hearing'* (Lk 4:21). Later, on the Mount of Beatitudes, before He began to spiritualise the Law of Moses, He would assert,

> Think not that I have come to abolish the law and the prophets; I have come not to abolish them but to fulfil them. For truly, I say to you, till heaven and earth pass away, not an iota, not a dot, will pass from the law until all is accomplished (Mt 5:17–18).

Then, as His conflict with the Jews over the observance of the Sabbath intensified, He would justify His actions by appealing to the Old Testament prophecies as they relate to Him: *'You search the scriptures, … and it is they that bear witness to me'* (Jn 5:39).

After His Resurrection, Christ met Cleopas and his companion on the road to Emmaus and chided them for being *'slow to believe all that the prophets had spoken'* about the Christ: *'And beginning with Moses and all the prophets, he interpreted to them in all the scriptures the things concerning himself'* (Lk 24:27).

Figure 3: *Christ and the two disciples on the road to Emmaus*

Equally, He intimated in His teachings that the expected Messianic kingdom was none other than the Church He would establish. Thus, He warned His disciples to expect to be calumniated in their governance of His Church: *'If they have called the master of the house Beelzebul, how much more will they malign those of his* household' (Mt 10:25). Later, He concluded His defence against the charge of being in league with demons by pointing out that *'if it is by the Spirit of God that I cast out demons, then the kingdom of God has come upon you'* (Mt 12:28).

At the Last Supper, Christ spoke to the Twelve about the kingdom, the Church, as being already present and, because of their loyalty, He gave them authority over it:

> You are those who have continued with me in my trials; and I assign to you, as my Father assigned to me, a kingdom, that you may eat and drink at my table in my kingdom, and sit on thrones judging the twelve tribes of Israel (Lk 22:28–30).

St Paul, likewise, spoke clearly to the Jewish community in Rome about the Church being the Messianic kingdom: *'And he expounded the matter to them from morning till evening, testifying to the kingdom of God and trying to convince them about Jesus both from the law of Moses and from the prophets.'* (Ac 28:23)

The Messianic Kingdom

The Old Testament prophecies outline several characteristics of the Messianic kingdom, the most significant being its catholicity or universal extent. The prophets foresaw the catholicity of the Messianic kingdom and foretold, not only the people of Israel, but also the Gentile nations would belong to the kingdom and serve the Messianic king. They also explicitly stated that all kings would serve and obey the Messiah and that the Messiah's dominion would extend to the ends of the earth.

I will tell of the decree of the Lord: He said to me,
　'You are my son, today I have begotten you.
Ask of me, and I will make the nations your heritage,
　and the ends of the earth your possession.
You shall break them with a rod of iron,
　and dash them in pieces like a potter's vessel.'
Now therefore, O kings, be wise; be warned,
　O rulers of the earth.
Serve the Lord with fear,
　with trembling
kiss his feet, lest he be angry,
　and you perish in the way;
for his wrath is quickly kindled.
　Blessed are all who take refuge in him (Ps 2:7–12).

Despite His power to break all opposition, the Messianic king is exceedingly humble and a man of peace, as the prophet Zechariah declared:

> Rejoice greatly, O daughter of Zion! Shout aloud, O daughter of Jerusalem! Lo, your king comes to you; triumphant and victorious is he, humble and riding on an ass, on a colt the foal of an ass. I will cut off the chariot from Ephraim and the war horse from Jerusalem; and the battle bow shall be cut off, and he shall command peace to the nations; his dominion shall be from sea to sea, and from the River to the ends of the earth (Zc 9:9–10).

The prophets also declared that the nations belonging to the kingdom would enjoy the intrinsic unity inherent to a common faith and a common worship. In particular, the prophets Micah and Isaiah, with great precision, declared the convergence of all peoples and nations to worship on the mountain of the house of the Lord:

> It shall come to pass in the latter days that the mountain of the house of the Lord shall be established as the highest of the mountains, and shall be raised up above the hills; and peoples shall flow to it, and many nations shall come, and say: 'Come, let us go up to the mountain of the Lord, to the house

of the God of Jacob; that he may teach us his ways and we may walk in his paths.' For out of Zion shall go forth the law, and the word of the Lord from Jerusalem (Mi 4:1–2; Is 2:2–3).

The abandonment of false gods and the united worship of the one, true God by all the inhabitants of the earth is to be the fruit of the Messiah's mission: '*And the Lord will become king over all the earth; on that day the Lord will be one and his name one*' (Zc 14:9).

The Messiah's triple office

The Messiah's triple office of Priest, Prophet and King is also clearly expounded in the Old Testament prophecies. His priesthood, first prefigured by Melchizedek's offering of bread and wine, was clearly seen and openly proclaimed by David: '*The Lord has sworn and will not change his mind, "You are a priest for ever after the order of Melchizedek"*' (Ps 110:4). There are three main points of resemblance between Melchizedek who is the prophetic type and Christ who fulfilled this prophecy. The points of resemblance are that both are kings as well as priests, that both offer bread and wine to God, and that both have their priesthood directly from God (Gn 14:18) and not through Aaron. Additionally, neither of them belongs to the tribe of Levi.

> For it is evident that our Lord was descended from Judah, and in connection with that tribe Moses said nothing about priests. This becomes even more evident when another priest arises in the likeness of Melchizedek, who has become a priest, not according to a legal requirement concerning bodily descent but by the power of an indestructible life (Heb 7:14–16).

Shortly before his death, Moses indicated to the people of Israel the importance of the Messiah's prophetic office. His function is not primarily to foretell the future, but to instruct and reprove the people in God's name. That Prophet would work miracles to establish His credentials. Consequently, Moses warned the people to listen attentively to the Prophet that God would raise up among them:

> The Lord your God will raise up for you a prophet like me from among you, from your brethren—him you shall heed—just as you desired of the Lord your God at Horeb on the day of the assembly, when you said, 'Let me not hear again the voice of the Lord my God, or see this great fire any more, lest I die.' And the Lord said to me, 'They have rightly said all that they have spoken. I will raise up for them a prophet like you from among their brethren; and I will put my words in his mouth, and he shall speak to them all that I command him. And whoever will not give heed to my words which he shall speak in my name, I myself will require it of him' (Dt 18:15–19).

The Israelites, throughout their history, lived in growing anticipation of that Prophet's advent. This expectation peaked with the appearance of John the Baptist at the Jordan, which induced the Jewish authorities to initiate a formal investigation by sending priests from Jerusalem to ask him, '*Are you the prophet?*' (Jn 1:21). The ordinary people also expected the Prophet to appear and, after the miracle of the five loaves, recognised him in Jesus, whom they now wanted to make king:

> When the people saw the sign which he had done, they said, 'This is indeed the prophet who is to come into the world!' Perceiving then that they were about to come and take him by force to make him king, Jesus withdrew again to the mountain by himself (Jn 6:14–15).

As he prepared for his death, the Patriarch '*Jacob called his sons, and said, "Gather yourselves together, that I may tell you what shall befall you in days to come"*' (Gn 49:1). Then, '*blessing each* [of his sons] *with the blessing suitable to him*' (Gn 49:28), Jacob blessed his son, Judah and foretold not only the Messiah's descent from him but also His kingly office, with its universal jurisdiction:

> Judah, your brothers shall praise you; your hand
> shall be on the neck of your enemies; your father's
> sons shall bow down before you. Judah is a lion's
> whelp; from the prey, my son, you have gone up.
> He stooped down, he couched as a lion, and as a
> lioness; who dares rouse him up? The sceptre shall
> not depart from Judah, nor the ruler's staff from
> between his feet, until he comes to whom it belongs;
> and to him shall be the obedience of the peoples (Gn
> 49:8–10).

The royal ancestry of the Messiah was definitively established when God chose David, a descendant of Judah, to be king over Israel and to rule from Jerusalem. In gratitude, David wished to build a Temple for God in Jerusalem but was prevented from doing so by God who promised him a son whose kingdom would last forever.

> When your days are fulfilled and you lie down with
> your fathers, I will raise up your offspring after you,
> who shall come forth from your body, and I will
> establish his kingdom. He shall build a house for my
> name, and I will establish the throne of his kingdom
> for ever. I will be his father, and he shall be my son.
> (2S 7:12–14)

With these words, God Himself renewed and confirmed Judah's prophecy regarding the Messiah's kingly office and everlasting kingdom.

The Old Testament prophecies about the Messianic kingdom stress three points that correlate with the Messiah's triple office. First, the Messianic kingdom will be endowed with a new and mystical sacrificial system; secondly, it will proclaim truths derived from divine revelation and thirdly, it will be governed by an authority emanating from the Messiah Himself.

New Sacrifice

With regard to the new sacrificial system, Ps 110:4 explicitly prophesied the priesthood of the Messiah, while predicting that the sacrifices of the Old Testament would be super-seded by the worship He would inaugurate. The prophet Isaiah, for example, spoke of the new priesthood, which was to be formed from among the Gentiles:

> I am coming to gather all nations and tongues; and they shall come and shall see my glory, and I will set a sign among them. And from them I will send survivors to the nations, to Tarshish, Put, and Lud, who draw the bow, to Tubal and Javan, to the coastlands afar off, that have not heard my fame or seen my glory; and they shall declare my glory among the nations. And they shall bring all your brethren from all the nations as an offering to the Lord, upon horses, and in chariots, and in litters, and upon mules, and upon dromedaries, to my holy mountain Jerusalem, says the Lord, just as the Israelites bring their cereal offering in a clean vessel to the house of the Lord. And some of them also I will take for priests and for Levites, says the Lord (Is 66:18–21).

The prophet Malachi, likewise, foretold the institution of a new sacrifice to be offered *'from the rising of the sun to its setting'* (Ml 1:11). According to Jeremiah, the sacrifice offered by the priesthood of the Messianic kingdom is to endure as long as day and night shall last:

> Thus says the Lord: If you can break my covenant with the day and my covenant with the night, so that day and night will not come at their appointed time, then also my covenant with David my servant may be broken, so that he shall not have a son to reign on his throne, and my covenant with the Levitical priests my ministers. As the host of heaven cannot be numbered and the sands of the sea cannot be measured, so I will multiply the descendants of

> David my servant, and the Levitical priests who
> minister to me (Jr 33:20–22).

The principle that a change in the priesthood necessarily
entails a change also in the laws of worship and sacrifice,
is confirmed in the Letter to the Hebrews: *'For when there is
a change in the priesthood, there is necessarily a change in the
law as well.'* (Heb 7:12) The reason for this lies in the intimate
connection between Covenant and priesthood, so much so
that a change in one necessitates a change in the other as
well. Attached to every Covenant are the laws and ordinances to be observed, the sacrifices to be offered, the days
on which to offer them and the feasts and festivals to be
kept. Consequently, when the Messiah brings in a new
Covenant, then all the laws relating the priesthood must
change, including what is to be sacrificed, when, how and
by whom. Specifically, the Messiah will replace the Levitical
Tribe that offered the Old Covenant animal sacrifices with
a new and royal priesthood offering a new sacrifice, no
longer on the Sabbath, which belongs to the Old Covenant,
but on the new day, the eighth day, the Lord's day, (Rev
1:10) which has no night.

New Covenant

The prophet Jeremiah attested that God would establish a
New Covenant in which greater and more personal divine
truths would be revealed:

> Behold, the days are coming, says the Lord, when I
> will make a new covenant with the house of Israel
> and the house of Judah, not like the covenant which
> I made with their fathers when I took them by the
> hand to bring them out of the land of Egypt, my
> covenant which they broke, ... But this is the cove-
> nant which I will make with the house of Israel after
> those days, says the Lord: I will put my law within
> them, and I will write it upon their hearts; and I will
> be their God, and they shall be my people. And no

> longer shall each man teach his neighbour and each
> his brother, saying, 'Know the Lord,' for they shall
> all know me, from the least of them to the greatest,
> says the Lord; for I will forgive their iniquity, and I
> will remember their sin no more (Jr 31:31–34).

Zechariah, likewise, declared that in the days of the Messiah, Jerusalem would be known as the city of truth: '*Thus says the Lord: I will return to Zion, and will dwell in the midst of Jerusalem, and Jerusalem shall be called the faithful city, and the mountain of the Lord of hosts, the holy mountain*' (Zc 8:3).

New Kingship

There are numerous passages in the Old Testament indicating that the kingdom would possess a new principle of authority arising from the personal rule of the Messiah. (Ps 2, Ps 71) The prophet Isaiah sums these up:

> For to us a child is born, to us a son is given; and the
> government will be upon his shoulder, and his name
> will be called 'Wonderful Counsellor, Mighty God,
> Everlasting Father, Prince of Peace.' Of the increase
> of his government and of peace there will be no end,
> upon the throne of David, and over his kingdom, to
> establish it, and to uphold it with justice and with
> righteousness from this time forth and for evermore.
> The zeal of the Lord of hosts will do this (Is 9:6–7).

Sometimes, the metaphor of a shepherd guiding and governing his flock is used in the Scriptures to describe the Messianic authority:

> And I will set up over them one shepherd, my
> servant David, and he shall feed them: he shall feed
> them and be their shepherd. And I, the Lord, will be
> their God, and my servant David shall be prince
> among them; I, the Lord, have spoken (Ezk 34:23–24).

Significantly, the prophecies relating to the priestly office image those of the kingly office. The prophets foretold the appointment of a priesthood, subordinate to the Messiah, as well as the Messiah's association of other 'shepherds' with Himself. Thus, the Messiah would exercise His authority over the nations through these shepherds delegated to govern in His name: '*I will cause your name to be celebrated in all generations; therefore the peoples will praise you for ever and ever*' (Ps 45:17).

Another characteristic of the kingdom would be the sanctity of its members. In the words of the prophet Isaiah: '*And a highway shall be there, and it shall be called the Holy Way; the unclean shall not pass over it, and fools shall not err therein*' (Is 35:8); and again, '*Awake, awake, put on your strength, O Zion; put on your beautiful garments, O Jerusalem, the holy city; for there shall no more come into you the uncircumcised and the unclean*' (Is 52:1).

Points to Remember

a. *The Old Testament prophecies outline the life and the work of the promised Messiah.*

b. *The Messiah would be a Priest, a Prophet and a King.*

c. *The Messiah would establish and rule over a universal or catholic kingdom that would embrace the entire human race united in a common faith and common worship.*

d. *The kingdom would be governed by shepherds delegated by the Messiah, would proclaim truths derived from divine revelation, and would have a priesthood that sanctifies its members.*

4

Christ did establish a Church

Preamble

It should first be noted that the writings of the New
Testament did not and, indeed, could not pre-exist the
Church Christ founded. Rather, New Testament is
primarily a record of some of the 'things which Jesus did'
(Jn 21:25) and of the founding, growth and activities of
His Church. Although numerous churches have been set
up based on certain Biblical passages and principles,
logically, they cannot be the Church Christ founded. It
will be shown from the Scriptures that Christ did
establish a visible Church to continue His work of
salvation and, that there are specific characteristics that
identify this Church. It is the promised kingdom of God
that fills the whole earth. It possesses an inherent capacity
for growth. It encompasses the whole human race and,
therefore, good and bad alike. The Church Christ
founded is not only a visible, inherently dynamic society
under the guidance of the Holy Spirit but, also a living
organism that has Christ as its life-generating principle.
In this sense, it is called the Mystical Body of Christ. While
the Church, with the assistance of the Holy Spirit, has the
divine mandate to teach the whole truth, nevertheless,
like Christ her head, she would experience opposition
and contradiction.

Exposition

Christ entered the world '*to gather into one the children of God who are scattered abroad*' (Jn 11:52). He gathered them into one Church, the word church being the English rendition of the Greek *ekklesia* (Latin *ecclesia*), a term used by the New Testament writers to denote the society founded by Jesus Christ. The Old Testament, employs two terms to describe the community of the children of Israel: *ecclesia* or church and synagogue. The former denotes the entire community of the children of Israel in their religious aspect, while the latter embraces the religious aspect in addition to other general gatherings of the Israelite community. The New Testament writers, however, drew a rigid distinction between the two terms: *ecclesia* was used to denote the Church of Christ while the Synagogue denoted the gatherings of the Jews who still adhere to the Old Covenant worship.

After His Sermon on the Mount of Beatitudes, Christ attracted many followers, called disciples. Then following a night in prayer, He chose from among these disciples twelve '*uneducated, common men*' (Ac 4:13), whom He called apostles; an apostle being '*one who is sent out*' (Lk 6:12). Christ associated the apostles very closely with Himself and His mission by sending them to '*preach the Kingdom of God and to heal*' (Lk 9:2) and also to share in His own authority to the extent that '*he who hears you hears me, and he who rejects you rejects me, and he who rejects me rejects him who sent me*' (Lk 10:16). Later, after His Resurrection from the dead, He would specifically confirm this appointment by telling them '*As the Father has sent me, even so I send you*' (Jn 20:21) and by giving them full authority to teach all nations '*to observe all that I have commanded you*' (Mt 28:20). The authority of the apostles was quite distinct from that of the rulers of the Synagogue who derived their authority from Moses. Christ, far from usurping the Mosaic authority, actually openly acknowledged it when He told the crowds and His disciples: '*the scribes and the Pharisees sit on Moses' seat; so practice and observe whatever they tell you, but not what they do; for they preach, but do not practice'* (Mt 23:2–3).

The kingdom of heaven

John the Baptist, *'of whom it is written, "Behold, I send my messenger before thy face, who shall prepare thy way before thee"'* (Mt 11:10), was the first person in Scripture to speak plainly of the kingdom of heaven: *'Repent, for the kingdom of heaven is at hand'* (Mt 3:2). His mission was to proclaim the imminence of the kingdom and to point to Jesus of Nazareth as the Messiah:

> The next day he saw Jesus coming toward him, and said, 'Behold, the Lamb of God, who takes away the sin of the world! This is he of whom I said, 'After me comes a man who ranks before me, for he was before me.' I myself did not know him; but for this I came baptising with water, that he might be revealed to Israel' (Jn 1:29–31).

Figure 4: *The preaching of John the Baptist*

After John's imprisonment, Christ began His public ministry with exactly the same words used by John *'Repent, for the kingdom of heaven is at hand'* (Mt 4:17). Later, when He sent the apostles out to preach on their own, He told them to go *'saying, 'The kingdom of heaven is at hand'* (Mt 10:7). The second petition of the Our Father, *'Thy kingdom come'* (Mt 6:10), underlines the centrality of the kingdom in Christ's mission and points to the importance of praying fervently for the coming of the *'kingdom prepared … from the foundation of the world'* (Mt 25:34). While the first petition directs our desire to the source of all glory, namely, God's holy name, the second arouses in us the hope of sharing in that glory by our becoming citizens of His kingdom.

The expression *'kingdom of heaven'* is used only in St Matthew's Gospel, probably because St Matthew wrote his Gospel for the Jews who, out of reverence, refrained from pronouncing the word *'God'*. The expression *'kingdom of God'*, however, is found in all four Gospels as well as in the Acts of the Apostles and the letters of St Paul. Christ used both expressions with the same meaning when He said to His disciples:

> Truly, I say to you, it will be hard for a rich man to enter the kingdom of heaven. Again I tell you, it is easier for a camel to go through the eye of a needle than for a rich man to enter the kingdom of God (Mt 19:23–24).

In addition, the kingdom of God refers not only to God's undisputed universal reign when all will be made new (Rev 21:5) but also to the Church, as will be shown below. Christ used many images and parables to describe this kingdom of God or of heaven.

The kingdom in parables

It is clear from several of the illustrations Christ used to describe the kingdom of heaven that on earth this kingdom embraces the entire human race, good and bad alike. In describing the kingdom as '*a net which was thrown into the sea and gathered fish of every kind*' (Mt 13:47), and as '*a field sown with good and bad seed*' (Mt 13:24–25), He teaches that, until the day of judgement, it will embrace both the good and the bad. This teaching becomes even clearer in the imagery of the true vine. There, Christ teaches that the good and bad are related to Him as branches to a vine and, that they receive the ministrations of the Father, according to their various dispositions: '*Every branch of mine that bears no fruit, he* (the Father) *takes away, and every branch that does bear fruit he prunes, that it may bear more fruit.*' (Jn 15:2) Therefore, while the good and the bad may well be indistinguishable in this life, their real identities will be revealed, with '*the coming of the Son of man. Then two men will be in the field; one is taken and one is left. Two women will be grinding at the mill; one is taken and one is left*' (Mt 24:39–41). Christ indicated that the day of judgment will be one for surprises:

> On that day many will say to me, 'Lord, Lord, did we not prophesy in your name, and cast out demons in your name, and do many mighty works in your name?' And then will I declare to them, 'I never knew you; depart from me, you evildoers' (Mt 7:22–23).

Since they profess faith in Christ by calling Him Lord and by using the charism of His name to cast out demons and to do mighty works, these evildoers were clearly citizens of the kingdom during their life in this world. However, their evil and unrepentant ways debar them from entry into eternal life and the permanent possession and enjoyment of the kingdom.

The kingdom of heaven possesses within itself a hidden inner dynamism for growth, expansion and fermentation. Christ illustrated these qualities by comparing it with

> a grain of mustard seed which a man took and sowed in his field; it is the smallest of all seeds, but when it has grown it is the greatest of shrubs and becomes a tree, so that the birds of the air come and

> make nests in its branches (Mt 13:31–32), and like
> leaven which a woman took and hid in three meas-
> ures of flour, till it was all leavened (Mt 13:33).

Christ explicitly taught that the kingdom of heaven would
embrace both good and bad as it grows and expands. He
also taught that it would be in the world, that it would be
visible and that it would have a distinct way of incorporating new members. Nicodemus was one of the first Pharisees
who recognised and acknowledged Christ's divine mission:

> Now there was a man of the Pharisees, named
> Nicodemus, a ruler of the Jews. This man came to
> Jesus by night and said to him, 'Rabbi, we know that
> you are a teacher come from God; for no one can do
> these signs that you do, unless God is with him' (Jn
> 3:1–2).

Christ immediately responded by speaking of the kingdom
and pointed out that to gain entrance into it a new birth was
required. Nicodemus interpreted this literally, so

> Jesus answered him, 'Truly, truly, I say to you,
> unless one is born anew, he cannot see the kingdom
> of God.' Nicodemus said to him, 'How can a man be
> born when he is old? Can he enter a second time into
> his mother's womb and be born?' (Jn 3:3–4).

Christ then clarified the matter with a declaration that entry
to the kingdom was gained through a spiritual rebirth in
Baptism:

> Jesus answered, 'Truly, truly, I say to you, unless
> one is born of water and the Spirit, he cannot enter
> the kingdom of God. That which is born of the flesh
> is flesh, and that which is born of the Spirit is spirit.
> Do not marvel that I said to you, 'You must be born
> anew' (Jn 3:5–7).

Nicodemus had come to Christ at night looking for a teacher
of divine truth but, unexpectedly, found a Saviour who
spoke to him about rebirth in Baptism, without which one
could not gain entry into the kingdom of God. His night

visit suggested he did not want to be publicly associated with Jesus, that is, he was not ready to make the sacrifice that entry into and possession of the kingdom entailed.

Later, Christ would illustrate with at least two parables the necessity of being ready to surrender everything for the sake of possessing the kingdom of God. In the first parable, the kingdom is encountered unexpectedly as a *'treasure hidden in a field, which a man found and covered up; then in his joy he goes and sells all that he has and buys that field'* (Mt 13:44). The labourer surrenders all his possessions in order to possess the great hidden wealth of the kingdom. In the second parable, *'the kingdom of heaven is like a merchant in search of fine pearls, who, on finding one pearl of great value, went and sold all that he had and bought it'* (Mt 13:45–46). Here, the kingdom is sought under the image of a pearl and the merchant is a connoisseur who is able to discern between pearls of varying quality. Like the labourer, he is prepared to exchange his great wealth for true riches. This stands in stark contrast with the rich young man who asked what he should do to inherit eternal life. *'Keep the commandments'* Jesus replied but, since the young man was really seeking perfection, Jesus said to him,

> 'One thing you still lack. Sell all that you have and distribute to the poor, and you will have treasure in heaven; and come, follow me.' But when he heard this he became sad, for he was very rich. Jesus looking at him said, 'How hard it is for those who have riches to enter the kingdom of God! For it is easier for a camel to go through the eye of a needle than for a rich man to enter the kingdom of God' (Lk 18:22–25).

His was a case of a divided heart, the story of one who wanted to serve both God and wealth, but *'No servant can serve two masters; for either he will hate the one and love the other, or he will be devoted to the one and despise the other. You cannot serve God and mammon'* (Lk 16:13). He went away sad, unable to make the sacrifice that membership of the kingdom demands.

Christ ended His teaching on the nature of the kingdom by asking the disciples whether they understood all He had said. Receiving an affirmative response, He then concluded *'every scribe who has been trained for the kingdom of heaven is like a householder who brings out of his treasure what is new and what is old'* (Mt 13:51–52).

He called the apostles scribes of the Church since whatever new things they preached in the Gospel, they would prove by referring to the old things as contained in the words of the Law and the Prophets. Thus, the Church founded by Christ on the apostles is the Bride who sings *'I have kept for you my beloved the new with the old.'* (Cant.7:13) The Song of Songs is an Old Testament poem about God's love for Israel, and prophetic of Christ's love for His Bride, the Church, whose full revelation will occur at the end of time when God will make all things new:

> Then I saw a new heaven and a new earth; for the first heaven and the first earth had passed away, and the sea was no more. And I saw the holy city, new Jerusalem, coming down out of heaven from God, prepared as a bride adorned for her husband (Rev 21:1–2).

Casting out Satan

John the Baptist was the first person to proclaim the imminence of the kingdom of heaven, a proclamation that Christ took up and expanded. When accused of casting out devils through the power of Beelzebul, Christ responded by asking the Pharisees rhetorically whether it was possible for any organisation to survive if it were divided against itself (Mt 12:22–27). With flawless logic, He concluded His defence with two unambiguous proclamations. First, He declared the palpable presence of the kingdom of heaven, *'But if it is by the Spirit of God that I cast out demons, then the* kingdom of God has come upon you' (Mt 12:28). Second, with another rhetorical question, He pronounced the overthrow of Satan whom He referred to as the strong man: *'how can one enter a strong man's house and plunder his goods, unless he first binds the strong man? Then indeed he may plunder his house'* (Mt 12:29).

In overcoming the first Adam, the devil not only entangled the whole human race in his rebellion against God, but also held the race in *'lifelong bondage.'*

Figure 5: *Adam and Eve are cast out of the Garden of Eden*

Christ, the second Adam, came to *'destroy him who has the power of death, that is, the devil'* (Heb 2:14), and to *'redeem us from all iniquity and to purify for himself a people of his own who are zealous for good deeds'* (Tt 2:14). Through His death and Resurrection, He gained victory over Satan and, as a result, was able to *'deliver all those who through fear of death were subject to lifelong bondage'* (Heb 2:15). Then, to ensure that His victory would be continuously attested, Christ promised to establish an indefectible Church that would preach and renew His victory throughout subsequent ages. This promise was made when He said to Simon Peter *'thou art Peter; and upon this rock I will build my church, and the gates of hell shall not prevail against it'* (Mt 16:18).

Figure 6: *Christ gives the keys to St Peter*

Now since *'whatever overcomes a man, to that he is enslaved'* (2P 2:19), it follows that every sin is a gate of hell. The question is sometimes raised as to whether Christ's promise means that the gates of hell should not prevail against the rock on which He built the Church or against the Church, which He built on the rock. The question raises a false dichotomy since clearly the gates of hell can prevail neither against the rock nor against the Church. That is, the Church would prove victorious over the gates of hell since Christ would endow it with power to free its members from every sin, and would build it on a rock that would never succumb to teaching any error since error, itself, leads to sin. Christ's promise is also a mandate for the Church to continue His warfare against error and sin. That is, the Church should not even wait to be attacked but should sally forth to conquer the gates of hell with the strength of Christ:

> For though we live in the world we are not carrying on a worldly war, for the weapons of our warfare are not worldly but have divine power to destroy strongholds. We destroy arguments and every proud obstacle to the knowledge of God, and take every thought captive to obey Christ, being ready to punish every disobedience, when your obedience is complete (2Co 10:3–7).

At the same time that Christ promised to build His Church on Peter, the rock, He conferred on this Church the gift of indefectibility, which means not merely that His Church would persist to the end of time but further, that it would preserve unimpaired its essential characteristics. In concrete terms, the promise that '*the gates of hell shall not prevail*' is an affirmation that, as a social organisation, the Church could never undergo any constitutional change that would make it something different from what it was originally. Specifically, as an institution founded by Jesus Christ, it could never become corrupt in faith or morals, although individual members and even its leaders, being human, may succumb to sin. Furthermore, this Church can never lose either its apostolic hierarchy or the sacraments through which Christ sanctifies or communicates grace to its members. These characteristics of the Church will be discussed later.

Visibility of the Kingdom

The kingdom has not only entered into this world but it has done so visibly as the *'city set on a hill cannot be hid'* (Mt 5:14). The kingdom of heaven on earth is the Church, *'built upon the foundation of the apostles and prophets, Christ Jesus himself being the cornerstone'* (Ep 2:20), and the sheepfold about which Christ said: *'other sheep have I that are not of this fold; I must bring them also, and they will heed my voice. So there shall be one flock, one shepherd'* (Jn 10:16).

It is *'God's building'* (1Co 3:9) built on rock, against which the gates of hell cannot prevail (Mt 16:18), and, most surprising, it is only *'through the church the manifold wisdom of God might now be made known to the principalities and powers in the heavenly places'* (Ep 3:10). This means, therefore, that the Church is instrumental in revealing to angels the *'breadth and length and height and depth'* (Ep 3:18) of the divine wisdom as St Peter also taught: *'It was revealed to them that ...the things which have now been announced to you by those who preached the good news to you through the Holy Spirit sent from heaven, things into which angels long to look'* (1P 1:12).

Adam's offence was not simply a personal sin. As the head of the human race, his trespass was an act with repercussions for the entire human race as St Paul made clear in his Letter to the Romans: *'sin came into the world through one man and death through sin, and so death spread to all men because all men sinned'* (Rm 5:12). Consequently, the entire human race was alienated from God by Adam's sin and could only be *'reconciled to God by the death of his Son'* (Rm 5:10). Thus, *'when the time had fully come, God sent forth his Son, born of woman, born under the law, to redeem those who were under the law, so that we might receive adoption as sons'* (Ga 4:4–5).

The Son of God, then, taking human nature from a virgin mother (Is 7:14) used His physical body as bait and a weapon to destroy the devil through whose *'envy death entered the world, and those who belong to his party experience it'* (Ws 2:24). Daniel's slaying of the Babylonian dragon is a prophetic anticipation of this:

> There was also a great dragon, which the Babylonians revered. And the king said to Daniel, 'You cannot deny that this is a living god; so worship him.' Daniel said, 'I will worship the Lord my God, for he is the living God. But if you, O king, will give me permission, I will slay the dragon without sword or club.' The king said, 'I give you permission.' Then Daniel took pitch, fat, and hair, and boiled them together and made cakes, which he fed to the dragon. The dragon ate them, and burst open. And Daniel said, 'See what you have been worshipping!' (Da 14:23–27).

Now *'the reason the Son of God appeared was to destroy the works of the devil'* (1Jn 3:8) and He achieved this when He rose from the dead after His physical body had been swallowed up by death. By incorporating His disciples as members of the Church He founded, Christ shares His victory over Satan with them, in such a way that His Church is more than a visible dynamic organisation. It is and will remain, in fact and above all, a living organism called His corporate or Mystical Body.

The Mystical Body

The Church, the Mystical Body of Christ, has Christ, Himself, not only as her head but also as her inner life-generating principle as He made clear in the metaphor *'I am the vine, you are the branches'* (Jn 15:5). Just as a branch receives life and nourishment from the vine, so the disciple, joined to Christ at Baptism and united to Him in His Mystical Body, receives Christ's own life. St Paul articulated this as *'it is no longer I who live, but Christ who lives in me; and the life I now live in the flesh I live by faith in the Son of God, who loved me and gave himself for me'* (Ga 2:20).

The second part of Jn 15:5 continues '*He who abides in me, and I in him, he it is that bears much fruit, for apart from me you can do nothing.*' It can be inferred from this verse that Christ's disciples abide in Him by believing, obeying and persevering, while He remains in them by enlightening, assisting and giving the grace of perseverance. Thus, union with Him is a consequence of the life of grace, that is, of avoiding sin and keeping His commandments as He emphatically taught, '*If you keep my commandments, you will abide in my love*' (Jn 15:10).

In Pauline thought, the Church is the body of Christ and its members belong to each other as much as they belong to Christ. St Paul expressed this reality when he wrote to the Romans '*For as in one body we have many members, and all the members do not have the same function, so we, though many, are one body in Christ, and individually members one of another*' (Rm 12:4–6). The inherent intimacy between Christ and His disciples is perhaps nowhere better grasped than in the Lord's rebuke of Saul for his persecution of the Church: '"*Saul, Saul, why do you persecute me?" And he said, "Who are you, Lord?" And he said, "I am Jesus, whom you are persecuting"*' (Ac 9:4–5). This exchange reveals that the bond between Christ and members of the Church He founded is as intimate as that of a man's soul with his body, so that if the body is injured the soul may well cry out '*you are hurting me*'. That is, whatever injury Saul the Pharisee inflicted on any member of the Mystical Body was inflicted on Christ Himself since '*If one member suffers, all suffer together; if one member is honoured, all rejoice together*' (1Co 12:26), from which it follows that, individually and collectively, the baptised make up the Mystical Body '*Now you are the body of Christ and individually members of it*' (1Co 12:27).

St Paul also declared to the Ephesians that the Father '*has made him* (Christ) *the head over all things for the church, which is his body*' (Ep 1:22–23), and has given gifts '*to equip the saints for the work of ministry, for building up the body of Christ*' (Ep 4:12). Using another image, St Paul also taught that the Church is Christ's spouse for whom He surrendered His life: '*Christ loved the church and gave himself up for her*' (Ep 5:25), and, as the bride of Christ, is a '*profound mystery*' (Ep 5:32). At the end of time, when Christ shall have purged her of her unfaithful members, she will be fully revealed in all her glory:

> Then came one of the seven angels who … spoke to me, saying, 'Come, I will show you the Bride, the wife of the Lamb.' And in the Spirit he carried me away to a great, high mountain, and showed me the holy city Jerusalem coming down out of heaven from God, having the glory of God, its radiance like a most rare jewel, like a jasper, clear as crystal. It had a great, high wall, with twelve gates, and at the gates twelve angels, and on the gates the names of the twelve tribes of the sons of Israel were inscribed; on the east three gates, on the north three gates, on the south three gates, and on the west three gates. And the wall of the city had twelve foundations, and on them the twelve names of the twelve apostles of the Lamb (Rev 21:9–14).

King Nebuchadnezzar in his dream, which only Daniel could interpret (Da 2), foresaw the Church, as the Mystical Body of Christ, that is, Christ as Head and the faithful as members, who hold '*fast to the Head, from whom the whole body, nourished and knit together through its joints and ligaments, grows with a growth that is from God*' (Col 2:19). The image of the '*stone … cut out by no human hand … that struck the image became a great mountain and filled the whole earth*' (Da 2:34–35) describes Christ the Virgin-born, as the stone, who in His members is a great mountain that fills the whole earth. Within this same imagery, the indefectible Church promised by Christ and built on rock fulfils the rest of Nebuchadnezzar's prophetic dream that

> the God of heaven will set up a kingdom which shall never be destroyed, nor shall its sovereignty be left to another people. It shall break in pieces all these kingdoms and bring them to an end, and it shall stand for ever (Da 2:44).

As the Mystical Body of Christ, the Church is the holy mountain of which Miriam, the sister of Moses prophetically sang after the people crossed the Red Sea: '*Thou wilt bring them in, and plant them on thy own mountain, the place, O Lord, which thou hast made for thy abode, the sanctuary, O Lord, which thy hands have established*' (Ex 15:17). Christ, the living stone, who said, '*No one can come to me unless the Father who sent me draws him*' (Jn 6:44) is her Head, and it is to Him that all members of His body are to conform as St Peter counselled:

> Come to him, to that living stone, rejected by men but in God's sight chosen and precious; and like living stones be yourselves built into a spiritual house, to be a holy priesthood, to offer spiritual sacrifices acceptable to God through Jesus Christ (1P 2:4–5).

Thus, the Father draws all the nations to the mountain of the Church where they make an acceptable spiritual offering in accordance with the declaration of the prophet Malachi:

> For from the rising of the sun to its setting my name is great among the nations, and in every place incense is offered to my name, and a pure offering; for my name is great among the nations, says the Lord of hosts (Ml 1:11).

Having previously taught the '*Jews who had believed in him, If you continue in my word, you are truly my disciples, and you will know the truth, and the truth will make you free*' (Jn 8:31–32), Christ, on the night He was betrayed, openly revealed Himself as '*the Truth*' (Jn 14:6). He was effectively saying that to obey His word was to know Him and that He would free all those who obey Him from their enslavement to sin.

> Jesus answered them, 'Truly, truly, I say to you, every one who commits sin is a slave to sin. The slave does not continue in the house for ever; the son

> continues for ever. So if the Son makes you free, you
> will be free indeed' (Jn 8:34–36).

It is not difficult to see that the house Christ mentioned refers to the Church, which in this world embraces good and bad alike. In this world, all within the Church struggle with sin: *'I do not understand my own actions. For I do not do what I want, but I do the very thing I hate'* (Rm 7:1). Christ, then, the Son who continues forever, promises true freedom and life to all who obey Him. *'Do you not know that if you yield yourselves to any one as obedient slaves, you are slaves of the one whom you obey, either of sin, which leads to death, or of obedience, which leads to righteousness?'* (Rm 6:16).

Truth

Christ commissioned His Church to continue the most important task of teaching the truth and to

> preach to the Gentiles the unsearchable riches of Christ, and to make all men see what is the plan of the mystery hidden for ages in God who created all things; that through the church the manifold wisdom of God might now be made known to the principalities and powers in the heavenly places (Ep 3:8–10).

Hence, even angels need the Church *'to comprehend with all the saints what is the breadth and length and height and depth'* (Ep 3:18) of God's plan of salvation.

The Apostles were to teach the truth, in the form of His commandments, (Jn 14:15) to all nations (Mt 28:20). For this task, He promised them the assistance of the Spirit of truth, *'the Counsellor, the Holy Spirit, whom the Father will send in my name, he will teach you all things, and bring to your remembrance all that I have said to you'* (Jn 14:26).

Fully aware that the Apostles were terrified because of His approaching crucifixion, Christ, wishing them to understand that truth is singular, indivisible and unique, told them that the Holy Spirit would teach the same truth as He Himself had:

> I have yet many things to say to you, but you cannot bear them now. When the Spirit of truth comes, he will guide you into all the truth; for he will not speak on his own authority, but whatever he hears he will speak, and he will declare to you the things that are to come. He will glorify me, for he will take what is mine and declare it to you (Jn 16:12–14).

In the Judgment of Solomon, the Spirit of truth had already taught that truth is both one and indivisible and, consequently, only one of two positions can be taken towards it.

> Then two harlots came to the king, and stood before him. The one woman said, 'Oh, my lord, this woman and I dwell in the same house; and I gave birth to a child while she was in the house. Then on the third day after I was delivered, this woman also gave birth; and we were alone; there was no one else with us in the house, only we two were in the house. And this woman's son died in the night, because she lay on it. And she arose at midnight, and took my son from beside me, while your maidservant slept, and laid it in her bosom, and laid her dead son in my bosom. When I rose in the morning to nurse my child, behold, it was dead; but when I looked at it closely in the morning, behold, it was not the child that I had borne.' But the other woman said, 'No, the living child is mine, and the dead child is yours.' The first said, 'No, the dead child is yours, and the living child is mine.' Thus they spoke before the king. Then the king said, 'The one says, 'This is my son that is alive, and your son is dead'; and the other says, 'No; but your son is dead, and my son is the living one.'' And the king said, 'Bring me a sword.' So a sword was brought before the king. And the king said, 'Divide the living child in two, and give half to the one, and half to the other.' Then the woman whose son was alive said to the king, because her heart yearned for her son, 'Oh, my lord, give her the living

> child, and by no means slay it.' But the other said,
> 'It shall be neither mine nor yours; divide it.' Then
> the king answered and said, 'Give the living child
> to the first woman, and by no means slay it; she is
> its mother' (1K 3:16–27).

Truth in many ways resembles a baby: it is one, it is whole, it is organic, it is unique and it cannot be divided. The baby's true mother would accept no compromise. Her maternal love is so intolerant that she must have the whole baby or nothing. But the false mother was unashamedly tolerant. She was willing to divide the baby; and the baby would have met its death through an act of broadmindedness. Truth, in a similar way, is preserved by intolerance of error and is most assuredly destroyed by compromise and broadmindedness.

While truth is singular and unique, error and falsehood are multiple since they appear in many different forms. Consequently and not surprisingly, Christ who is Truth encountered contradiction throughout His public life (Lk 2:34) and, was not only called a deceiver (Mt 27:63) but, was also accused of being in league with demons (Jn 11:47–48; Mk 3:22). Since the Church is His Body and all members suffer the same thing, Christ warned His disciples that they should not expect her to be treated any differently:

> If the world hates you, know that it has hated me
> before it hated you. If you were of the world, the
> world would love its own; but because you are not
> of the world, but I chose you out of the world,
> therefore the world hates you. Remember the word
> that I said to you, 'A servant is not greater than his
> master.' If they persecuted me, they will persecute
> you; if they kept my word, they will keep yours also
> (Jn 15:18–21; see also Mt 10:17–23; Lk 23:31).

So from the beginning of their apostolate, the Apostles concentrated on preaching and teaching (Ac 6:2–4, 1Tm 4:11–13) and were constantly on their guard to protect the faithful against the appearance of error (2Tm 3:8). For example, St Paul made a point of counselling Timothy to follow the pattern of the sound words which you have heard from me, in the faith and love which are in Christ Jesus; guard the truth that has been entrusted to you by the Holy Spirit who dwells within us (2Tm 1:13–14).

When Christ gave Simon Peter and the other Apostles the power to bind and loose, He effectively established His Church not only as the *'the pillar and bulwark of the truth'* (1Tm 3:15) but also as the tribunal of final appeal. Christ had, in fact, instructed His disciples that they should resolve any differences between themselves but if the offender proved obdurate, then the aggrieved party was to *'tell it to the church; and if he refuses to listen even to the church, let him be to you as a Gentile and a tax collector. Truly, I say to you, whatever you bind on earth shall be bound in heaven, and whatever you loose on earth shall be loosed in heaven'* (Mt 18:17–18).

Points to Remember

a. *Christ promised that He would establish an indefectible Church.*

b. *The Church is the promised kingdom of God, foretold by the Prophets.*

c. *Christ chose twelve Apostles whom He sent out into the world to proclaim the presence of the kingdom of heaven.*

d. *Christ empowered His Apostles to speak and act in His name and by His authority.*

e. *Membership to the Church is attained through Baptism.*

f. *The Church possesses an inherent capacity for growth and expansion.*

g. *The Church possesses the gift of indefectibility, that is, she will endure with her essential characteristics unimpaired until the end of time.*

h. *The Church is a visible dynamic society that embraces the whole human race, good and bad alike.*

i. *The Church is a living organism that has Christ as her life principle; she is His Mystical Body and her members are intimately united to Him and to each other.*

j. *As the 'pillar and bulwark of the truth', the Church has the divine mandate to teach all nations those truths necessary for salvation but, like Christ her head, she experiences opposition and contradiction.*

5

The Mission of the Church Christ founded

Preamble

God's love for His creation is unconditional. He proved the greatness of His love when He sent His only-begotten Son, Jesus Christ, on the mission to redeem fallen creation. Christ fulfilled this mission of redemption by His life, death and Resurrection. In order for this redemption to be applied to future generations, He entrusted His own mission to the Church. He organised the Church with a visible head, Simon Peter, with the Holy Spirit as her animating principle and with a promise of His own continuing Presence as a guarantee of her indefectibility. Spread throughout the world, the Church remains a single entity even when she manifests herself as a household, or as a community, whether civic or regional, or as a universal society. The Church's mission is not in addition to that of Christ and the Holy Spirit but, rather, the outward manifestation and continuing expression of it. In her whole being and in all her members, the Church Christ founded is sent to announce, to bear witness, to make present and to distribute the fruits of the mysteries of the divine self-disclosure to the human race.

Exposition

Despite being corrupted by sin, creation remains good and Scripture affirms that God has an abiding love for it: *'For thou lovest all things that exist, and hast loathing for none of the things, which thou hast made, for thou wouldst not have made anything if thou hadst hated it'* (Ws 11:24).

Christ explained to Nicodemus the strategy God had adopted to rescue the human race from sin and death. It was nothing less than His Son should *'give his life as a ransom for many'* (Mt 20:28) and grant eternal life to all those who believe in Him: *'For God so loved the world that he gave his only Son, that whoever believes in him should not perish but have eternal life'* (Jn 3:16).

In His desire for *'all men to be saved and to come to the knowledge of the truth'* (1Tm 2:4), God entrusted to His only Son a mission. Christ explained this mission as follows:

> For I have come down from heaven, not to do my own will, but the will of him who sent me; and this is the will of him who sent me, that I should lose nothing of all that he has given me, but raise it up at the last day (Jn 6:38–39).

The Father sent His Son on a mission: *'The reason the Son of God appeared was to destroy the works of the devil'* (1Jn 3:8). He initiated His mission in the Synagogue at Nazareth:

> And he came to Nazareth, … went to the synagogue, … stood up to read; … opened the book and found the place where it was written, 'The Spirit of the Lord is upon me, because he has anointed me to preach good news to the poor. He has sent me to proclaim release to the captives and recovering of sight to the blind, to set at liberty those who are oppressed, to proclaim the acceptable year of the Lord.' And he closed the book, … sat down; and the eyes of all in the synagogue were fixed on him. And he began to say to them, 'Today this scripture has been fulfilled in your hearing' (Lk 4:16–2).

Then leaving Nazareth, '*He went about doing good and healing all that were oppressed by the devil, for God was with him*' (Ac 10:38). The mission He received from His Father would be completed on Calvary, when He not only '*gave himself for us to redeem us from all iniquity and to purify for himself a people of his own who are zealous for good deeds,*' (Tt 2:14) but also '*destroyed him who has the power of death, that is, the devil, and delivered all those who through fear of death were subject to lifelong bondage*' (Heb 2:14–16).

On the night of His betrayal, with His mission drawing towards its conclusion, the Lord Jesus, in His high priestly prayer to His Father, reviewed His mission. He prayed '*I glorified thee on earth, having accomplished the work which thou gavest me to do; and now, Father, glorify thou me in thy own presence with the glory which I had with thee before the world was made*' (Jn 17:4–5). On Calvary, He declared His mission complete with the words '*It is finished*' (Jn 19:30). All that remained now was for the fruits of His work of redemption to be applied to future generations. Acting in His name and with His power, this would be the task of the Apostles whom He had chosen and the mission of the Church that He had founded.

The Apostles continue Christ's mission

At the beginning of His public life, and after a night of prayer, Christ chose His twelve Apostles and trained them over a three-year period. Before suffering His passion and death, He prayed to His Father for the apostles whom He would send into the world '*As thou didst send me into the world, so I have sent them into the world.*' (Jn 17:18) Then, after His Resurrection from the dead, He entrusted them with a mission that was, in all essentials, His own, when He told them '*As the Father has sent me, even so I send you*' (Jn 20:21). Thus, the mission the Father had given Him was to be continued through the ministry of the Apostles, who '*went forth and preached everywhere, while the Lord worked with them* and confirmed the message by the signs that attended it' (Mk 16:20).

Empowering His Apostles with the promise of His continuing presence, Christ commanded them to preach and teach the Gospel to every creature:

> Go therefore and make disciples of all nations, baptising them in the name of the Father and of the Son and of the Holy Spirit, teaching them to observe all that I have commanded you; and lo, I am with you always, to the close of the age (Mt 28:19).

Figure 7: *The Ascension of Christ*

Through preaching, unbelievers are brought to faith and then they are perfected in faith by the apostolic teaching so that the words of the prophet Joel might be fulfilled *'all who call on the name of the Lord shall be delivered'* (Jl 2:32). The phrase *'The Lord be with you'* is used at least ninety times in the Bible, and outside of the few instances in which it implies a simple salutation (Rt 2:4; Rm 15:33), it signifies that God will ensure the success of the person's undertaking (Gn 39:2; Ex 3:12; Jr 1:19; Num 14:42). Before He ascended into heaven, the Lord Jesus promised *'I am with you always, to the close of the age'* (Mt 28:20) guaranteeing the Apostles' success in preaching the Gospel to every creature throughout time until His second coming on Judgement Day.

St Paul, who was *'appointed a preacher and apostle and teacher'* (2Tm 1:11), recognised that not only must knowledge of God precede the invocation of His name but, also, that the authenticity of this knowledge could only be guaranteed when it was delivered by those authorised to preach it. Hence, he wrote the Romans:

> But how are men to call upon him in whom they have not believed? And how are they to believe in him of whom they have never heard? And how are they to hear without a preacher? And how can men preach unless they are sent? … So faith comes from what is heard, and what is heard comes by the preaching of Christ (Rm 10:14–17).

St Paul regarded the preaching of the Gospel as so important that he even rejoiced when those preaching it did so with mixed motives:

> Some indeed preach Christ from envy and rivalry, but others from good will. The latter do it out of love, knowing that I am put here for the defence of the gospel; the former proclaim Christ out of partisanship, not sincerely but thinking to afflict me in my imprisonment. What then? Only that in every way, whether in pretence or in truth, Christ is proclaimed; and in that I rejoice (Phil.1:15–18).

No doubt, he was fully confident that the Lord Jesus who said, *'Not every one who says to me, 'Lord, Lord,' shall enter the kingdom of heaven'* (Mt 7:21), on the day of His visitation, would *'render to every man according to his works'* (Rm 2:6).

Since nothing unclean shall enter the heavenly Jerusalem, (Rev 21:27) Christ, at the beginning of His public ministry, indicated the goal towards which His disciples should strive: *'You, therefore, must be perfect, as your heavenly Father is perfect'* (Mt 5:48). He then set about making them perfect or holy by forgiving them their sins and exhorting them to sin no more. He demonstrated that He had the authority to forgive sin by freeing the paralytic from his infirmity: *'But that you may know that the Son of man has authority on earth to forgive sins — he then said to the paralytic — 'Rise, take up your bed and go home.' And he rose and went home'* (Mt 9:6–7). Christ warned another paralytic whom He had cured, *'See, you are well! Sin no more, that nothing worse befall you.'* (Jn 5:14) He also forgave the sins of the woman in the house of Simon the Pharisee: *'I tell you, her sins, which are many, are forgiven'* (Lk 7:47). He did the same for the woman caught in adultery, saying *'Neither do I condemn you; go, and do not sin again'* (Jn 8:11). Zacchaeus likewise received forgiveness *'Jesus said to him, "Today salvation has come to this house, since he also is a son of Abraham"'* (Lk 19:9). The most blessed of all His penitents, however, was the thief on the cross who received forgiveness as well as the promise of imminent and full redemption *'Truly, I say to you, today you will be with me in Paradise'* (Lk 23:43).

Since the Son *'of God has appeared for the salvation of all men, training us to renounce irreligion and worldly passions, and to live sober, upright, and godly lives in this world'* (Tt 2:11–12), the Apostles' mission, likewise, must include the sanctification of the faithful. The Apostles would carry out their mission of sanctifying the faithful by administering the sacraments instituted by Christ and so reap the fruit that would last: *'You did not choose me, but I chose you and appointed you that you should go and bear fruit and that your fruit should abide'* (Jn 15:16).

The Sacraments

Christ's mission consisted in carrying out the work of redemption (Ep 1:7), that is, to free the human race from sin and from Satan's clutches by the power of His death and Resurrection (Col 1:13). The mission of the Church He founded would be to offer the fruits of redemption to individual souls by means of seven visible signs, which He instituted. In doing this, Christ took into account the fact that it is impossible to keep people together in one religious denomination, whether true or false, unless they are united by means of visible signs or sacraments. The sacraments Christ instituted, then, are holy signs that have power to transmit grace and so sanctify their recipients, even as His cloak was the tangible means by which the woman with the haemorrhage was healed.

> And there was a woman who had had a flow of blood for twelve years, ... She had heard the reports about Jesus, and came up behind him in the crowd and touched his garment. For she said, 'If I touch even his garments, I shall be made well.' And immediately the haemorrhage ceased; and she felt in her body that she was healed of her disease. And Jesus, perceiving in himself that power had gone forth from him, immediately turned about in the crowd, and said, 'Who touched my garments?' ... And he looked around to see who had done it. But the woman, knowing what had been done to her, came in fear and trembling and fell down before him, and told him the whole truth. And he said to her, 'Daughter, your faith has made you well; go in peace, and be healed of your disease' (Mk 5:25–34).

Although not all seven sacraments are named explicitly in Scripture, each sacrament is, nonetheless, identifiable by what it signifies and by the fact that it is administered with apostolic mandate, as the following will show.

The Sacrament of Baptism

The first of the seven sacraments instituted by Christ is Baptism. Together with the sacraments of Confirmation and the Holy Eucharist, Baptism constitutes the sacraments of Christian initiation. After His Resurrection, Christ specifically commanded His Apostles to *'go and make disciples of all nations, baptizing them in the name of the Father and of the Son and of the Holy Spirit'* (Mt 28:19). The Acts of the Apostles record that from the very day of Pentecost the Church has celebrated and administered the Sacrament of Baptism through which all sins are forgiven. *'Peter said to them, "Repent, and be baptised every one of you in the name of Jesus Christ for the forgiveness of your sins; and you shall receive the gift of the Holy Spirit"'* (Ac 2:38). Further, according to the teachings of St Paul, the baptised enter into communion with Christ's death, are buried with Him, and rise with Him:

> Do you not know that all of us who have been baptized into Christ Jesus were baptized into his death? We were buried therefore with him by baptism into death, so that as Christ was raised from the dead by the glory of the Father, we too might walk in newness of life. (Rm 6:3–4)

Thus, through the Holy Spirit and the bath that purifies, sanctifies and justifies, the baptised, in addition to putting on Christ (Ga 3:27), also receive a new kind of life: *'But you were washed, you were sanctified, you were justified in the name of the Lord Jesus Christ and in the Spirit of our God'* (1Co 6:11).

The waters of Baptism symbolise not only death and burial, but also purification, regeneration and renewal. Baptism has two principal effects, namely, purification from sins and a new birth in the Holy Spirit: *'Jesus answered, "Truly, truly, I say to you, unless one is born of water and the Spirit, he cannot enter the kingdom of God"'* (Jn 3:5). Through

Baptism, all sins, original and personal, as well as all punishment due to sin are forgiven. Although Baptism destroys all that would impede the entry of the baptised into the kingdom of God, it does not eliminate the temporal consequences of sin such as suffering, sickness and death, nor does it remove the inherent weaknesses of character, or the inclination to sin of which St Paul complained:

> For I know that nothing good dwells within me, that is, in my flesh. I can will what is right, but I cannot do it. For I do not do the good I want, but the evil I do not want is what I do. Now if I do what I do not want, it is no longer I that do it, but sin which dwells within me. So I find it to be a law that when I want to do right, evil lies close at hand. For I delight in the law of God, in my inmost self, but I see in my members another law at war with the law of my mind and making me captive to the law of sin which dwells in my members. Wretched man that I am! Who will deliver me from this body of death? Thanks be to God through Jesus Christ our Lord! So then, I of myself serve the law of God with my mind, but with my flesh I serve the law of sin (Rm 7:18–25).

Therefore, holding fast to Christ's victory, the Christian must engage in the struggle against sin even to the point of death (Heb 12:4), since '*an athlete is not crowned unless he competes according to the rules*' (2Tm 2:5).

Baptism not only purifies from all sin but also, by conferring sanctifying grace on the soul, makes it a friend of God (Jn 15:14), an adopted child of God (Rm 8:15) and, even more, a partaker of the divine nature (2P 1:4). Further, it imparts the virtues of faith, hope and charity (1Co 13:13) and transforms the person baptised into a living temple of the Holy Spirit (1Co 6:19). Baptism is a second birth (Jn 3:5) that reconciles the baptised with the Father and configures them to Christ '*For as many of you as were baptised into Christ have put on Christ*' (Ga 3:27), as it incorporates them as members of His Mystical Body: '*For by one Spirit we were all baptised into one body*' (1Co 12:13).

Infant Baptism

Since there is no explicit mention of infants being baptised in the New Testament, there is, consequently, no prohibition of it. Nonetheless, the New Testament does record that St Paul baptised whole families, which may well have included infants (Ac 16:15; 16:33; 18:8; 1Co 1:16). Likewise, St Peter baptised not only Cornelius but also *'his kinsmen and close friends'* (Ac 10:23) who had been invited. Additionally, Christ sent the Apostles to teach and baptise all nations, which certainly includes children and not just adult men and women.

Figure 8: *St Peter baptizes Cornelius*

St Paul also taught that all Adam's descendants inherited his condition and so *'were by nature children of wrath'* (Ep 2:3). Specifically, in much the same way that Levi *'paid tithes through Abraham, for he was still in the loins of his ancestor when Melchizedek met him'* (Heb 7:9–10), so also, because the entire human race was still in Adam's loins, *'many were made sinners'* (Rm 5:19) by Adam's disobedience. Thus, all Adam's descendants share in his sin as the prophet-king declared, *'Behold, I was brought forth in iniquity, and in sin did my mother conceive me'* (Ps 51:5). Children, even though incapable of personal sin, nevertheless, inherit the moral condition of Adam, the head and father of the human race: *'for in Adam all die'* (1Co 15:22).

Infant Baptism is, therefore, necessary because infants have contracted, through no fault of their own, the guilt of original sin, which *'the free gift'* of Baptism alone can remit (Jn 3:5). The principal effect of Adam's sin is death, which Christ cancels by conferring eternal life through the waters of Baptism: *'If, because of one man's trespass, death reigned through that one man, much more will those who receive the abundance of grace and the free gift of righteousness reign in life through the one man Jesus Christ'* (Rm 5:17). If Baptism then can forgive sin and confer an abundance of grace on the worst of sinners, much more would it benefit the infant as the sin forgiven is not his own but that of another. The necessity and validity of infant baptism also follows naturally from Ezekiel's prophetic utterance that re-established the teaching regarding individual and personal responsibility for sin.

> The soul that sins shall die. The son shall not suffer for the iniquity of the father, nor the father suffer for the iniquity of the son; the righteousness of the righteous shall be upon himself, and the wickedness of the wicked shall be upon himself (Ezk 18:20).

Now, infants are born in a state of sin for which they are not personally responsible because *'one man's trespass led to condemnation for all men'*. Therefore, since *'one man's act of righteousness leads to acquittal and life for all men'* (Rm 5:18), infants may obtain salvation through a spiritual rebirth in the waters of Baptism, because *'there is ... now no condemnation for those who are in Christ Jesus'* (Rm 8:1).

The spiritual regeneration brought about by Baptism is comparable to physical birth. The child, while in the mother's womb, does not receive nourishment independently but through the agency of its mother. Hence, also children before the use of reason, being as it were in the womb of their mother, the Church, receive salvation not by their own act but by the action of the Church. Thus, in the same way that circumcision of Jewish infants signified entry into the Old Covenant, so its fulfilment, Baptism, introduces infants into the New Covenant people of God.

> In him also you were circumcised with a circumcision made without hands, by putting off the body of flesh in the circumcision of Christ; and you were buried with him in baptism, in which you were also raised with him through faith in the working of God, who raised him from the dead. And you, who were dead in trespasses and the uncircumcision of your flesh, God made alive together with him, having forgiven us all our trespasses, having cancelled the bond which stood against us with its legal demands; this he set aside, nailing it to the cross (Col 2:11–14).

The Sacrament of Confirmation

The prophet Isaiah foretold that the Spirit of the Lord would rest on the promised Messiah to consecrate Him for His saving mission:

> There shall come forth a shoot from the stump of Jesse, and a branch shall grow out of his roots. And the Spirit of the Lord shall rest upon him, the spirit of wisdom and understanding, the spirit of counsel and might, the spirit of knowledge and the fear of the Lord. And his delight shall be in the fear of the Lord (Is 11:1–3).

The people of Israel lived in expectation of the Messiah's advent and flocked to the Jordan to be baptised by John the Baptist. John, however, openly declared to his disciples '*You yourselves bear me witness, that I said, I am not the Christ, but I have been sent before him*' (Jn 3:28). On the other hand, when Christ came to the Jordan, John proclaimed Him '*Behold, the*

Lamb of God, who takes away the sin of the world!' (Jn 1:29). He had previously testified that

> I saw the Spirit descend as a dove from heaven, and it remained on him. I myself did not know him; but he who sent me to baptize with water said to me, 'He on whom you see the Spirit descend and remain, this is he who baptizes with the Holy Spirit.' And I have seen and have borne witness that this is the Son of God (Jn 1:32–34).

The descent of the Holy Spirit on the Lord Jesus at His Baptism was a sign that this was *'he who is to come'* (Mt 11:3), the Messiah, the Son of God. According to the prophet Joel, as authoritatively interpreted by St Peter at Pentecost, (Ac 2:14–16) the outpouring of the Spirit was for all:

> And it shall come to pass afterward, that I will pour out my spirit on all flesh; your sons and your daughters shall prophesy, your old men shall dream dreams, and your young men shall see visions. Even upon the menservants and maidservants in those days, I will pour out my spirit. (Jl 2:28–29)

Christ repeatedly promised the Holy Spirit to those who believe in Him but nowhere more forcefully than at the Feast of Tabernacles when He *'stood up and proclaimed, "If any one thirst, let him come to me and drink. He who believes in me, as the scripture has said, 'Out of his heart shall flow rivers of living water'"* (Jn 7:37–38). By way of explanation, St John commented, *'Now this he said about the Spirit, which those who believed in him were to receive; for as yet the Spirit had not been given, because Jesus was not yet glorified'* (Jn 7:39). On the night of His betrayal, with His glorification just hours away, He consoled His apostles with the promise of the gift of the Holy Spirit, who would be an Advocate (Jn 15:26) and the Revealer of divine truth (Jn 16:8–14) to them. Shortly before His Ascension into heaven, He instructed His apostles to *'stay in the city, until you are clothed with power from on high'* (Lk 22:49). This clothing took place at Pentecost when the Holy Spirit descended to confirm and to strengthen them for the task of proclaiming the death and Resurrection of the Lord

> Men of Israel, hear these words: Jesus of Nazareth, a man attested to you by God with mighty works and wonders and signs which God did through him in your midst, as you yourselves know— this Jesus, delivered up according to the definite plan and foreknowledge of God, you crucified and killed by the hands of lawless men. But God raised him up, having loosed the pangs of death, because it was not possible for him to be held by it (Ac 2:22–24).

Figure 9: *St Peter on the day of Pentecost*

All Christ's disciples are destined to receive this Pentecostal gift as St John explained (Jn 7:38) and St Peter confirmed, *'you shall receive the gift of the Holy Spirit'* (Ac 2:38).

The sacrament of Confirmation, which, by the conferral of the Holy Spirit, completes baptismal grace, is alluded to in several places in the New Testament under the image of a seal. Since salvation is effected *'by the washing of regeneration and renewal in the Holy Spirit'* (Tt 3:5), St Paul declared that God *'has put his seal upon us and given us his Spirit in our hearts as a guarantee'* (2Co 1:21–22). He reminded the Ephesians that they *'were sealed with the promised Holy Spirit, which is the guarantee of our inheritance until we acquire possession of it'* (Ep 1:13–14). St John, recalling Christ's promise of the Spirit who would lead to the complete truth, wrote, *'you have been anointed by the Holy One'* (1Jn 2:20), so that

> the anointing which you received from him abides in you, and you have no need that anyone should teach you; as his anointing teaches you about everything, and is true, and is no lie, just as it has taught you, abide in him. (1Jn 2:27)

Somewhat less dramatically, but nonetheless with the same power and effect to confirm and to strengthen, the Church confers the gift of the Holy Spirit on her members in the sacrament of Confirmation by the laying-on of hands. The New Testament records that only an Apostle or one of his successors could impart this sacrament, which is quite distinct from Baptism. Hence, if the baptiser were an Apostle he would immediately confer the sacrament of Confirmation to the persons baptised, as St Paul did at Corinth where believers were first baptised and then confirmed by the laying-on of his hands: *'On hearing this, they were baptised in the name of the Lord Jesus. And when Paul had laid his hands upon them, the Holy Spirit came on them; and they spoke with tongues and prophesied'* (Ac 19:5–6).

When, however, the baptiser was not an Apostle, the baptised persons had to wait for the visit of an Apostle as is explicitly related of the Samaritans:

> Now when the apostles at Jerusalem heard that
> Samaria had received the word of God, they sent to
> them Peter and John, who came down and prayed
> for them that they might receive the Holy Spirit; for
> it had not yet fallen on any of them, but they had
> only been baptised in the name of the Lord Jesus.
> Then they laid their hands on them and they
> received the Holy Spirit (Ac 8:14–17).

The laying-on of hands was not the only means by which
extraordinary gifts were bestowed. This is proven by the
fact that there were occasions when these gifts were given
without any external rite, such as the laying-on of hands

> While Peter was still saying this, the Holy Spirit fell
> on all who heard the word. And the believers from
> among the circumcised who came with Peter were
> amazed, because the gift of the Holy Spirit had been
> poured out even on the Gentiles (Ac 10:44–45).

Equally, not all gifts were bestowed with the conferral of
the sacrament of Confirmation '*Do all possess gifts of healing?
Do all speak with tongues? Do all interpret?*' (1Co 12:30). The
sacrament of Confirmation is essentially for the inner
strengthening of the Holy Spirit to make Christians mature
and soldiers of Christ ready to profess and defend their faith
in Him (1Co 13:11; 1Co 15:10; 2Co 12:9).

The Sacrament of the Holy Eucharist

At the Last Supper, on the night He was betrayed, the Lord
Jesus instituted the Eucharistic Sacrifice of His Body and
Blood. This Eucharist, the Lord's Supper is a sacrament as
well as a sacrifice. As a sacrament, it contains the real Body
and Blood of Christ under the sign of bread and wine. As
a sacrifice, it makes present in time and space the one single
sacrifice Christ offered on Calvary.

In the Synagogue at Capernaum, Christ called Himself
the Bread of life and promised to give His Flesh as food and

His Blood as drink that those partaking of It may not die but live forever.

> I am the bread of life. Your fathers ate the manna in the wilderness, and they died. This is the bread which comes down from heaven, that a man may eat of it and not die. I am the living bread which came down from heaven; if any one eats of this bread, he will live for ever; and the bread which I shall give for the life of the world is my flesh (Jn 6:48–51).

The Jews understood Him literally and started looking for ways in which His saying could be interpreted symbolically. Christ, however, merely repeated six more times what He had said. Each repetition was more explicit and forceful than the last so that only a literal interpretation was possible.

> The Jews then disputed among themselves, saying, 'How can this man give us his flesh to eat?' So Jesus said to them, 'Truly, truly, I say to you, unless you eat the flesh of the Son of man and drink his blood, you have no life in you; he who eats my flesh and drinks my blood has eternal life, and I will raise him up at the last day. For my flesh is food indeed, and my blood is drink indeed. He who eats my flesh and drinks my blood abides in me, and I in him. As the living Father sent me, and I live because of the Father, so he who eats me will live because of me. This is the bread which came down from heaven, not such as the fathers ate and died; he who eats this bread will live for ever' (Jn 6:52–58).

The consequence of the literalness of His teaching was that *'Many of his disciples, when they heard it, said, "This is a hard saying; who can listen to it?"'* (Jn 6:60). Christ, however, refused to modify His teaching or to allow for any but a literal interpretation and so *'After this many of his disciples drew back and no longer went about with him'* (Jn 6:66).

At the Last Supper, Christ fulfilled His promise to give His Flesh as food and His Blood as drink.

> And he took bread, and when he had given thanks
> he broke it and gave it to them, saying, 'This is my
> body which is given for you. Do this in remembrance
> of me.' And likewise the cup after supper, saying,
> 'This cup which is poured out for you is the new
> covenant in my blood' (Lk 22:19–20).

Thus, in the Eucharist, under the appearances of bread and
wine, Christ is present, whole and entire, Body, Blood, Soul
and Divinity. St Paul explicitly taught this doctrine of
Christ's Real Presence in the Eucharist: *'The cup of blessing
which we bless, is it not a participation in the blood of Christ?
The bread which we break, is it not a participation in the body of
Christ?'* (1Co 10:16) and its corollary:

> Whoever, therefore, eats the bread or drinks the cup
> of the Lord in an unworthy manner will be guilty of
> profaning the body and blood of the Lord. Let a man
> examine himself, and so eat of the bread and drink
> of the cup. For anyone who eats and drinks without
> discerning the body eats and drinks judgment upon
> himself (1Co 11:27–29).

The Eucharist, as a sacrifice, is a memorial of the death and
Resurrection of Christ. On the night of His betrayal, Christ
offered Himself as a victim for sin to His heavenly Father
under the appearances of bread and wine as a sacrifice for
sin. By consecrating the bread and wine separately, He
clearly manifested the bloody separation of His body and
soul on the cross. Furthermore, He left this visible unbloody
sacrifice to His Church and He commanded His Apostles
to offer this same sacrifice *'from the rising of the sun to its
setting'* (Ml 1:10–11) with the words *'Do this in remembrance
of me'* (Lk 22:19).

Thus, the Eucharistic Sacrifice is the means established
by Christ to impart the saving power of the cross for the
remission of sins throughout the ages. It not only makes
present His victory over sin, death and Satan but also
provides the food whereby His disciples may be intimately
united with Him. *'Lord, to whom shall we go? You have the*

words of eternal life; and we have believed, and have come to know, that you are the Holy One of God' (Jn 6:54–56).

The Sacrament of Reconciliation

Adam was brought into being and the whole human race with him, in much the same way that Levi was in the loins of his great grandfather, Abraham (Heb 7:9). Adam sinned and all, by sharing in his nature, sinned with him: *'Therefore as sin came into the world through one man and death through sin, and so death spread to all men because all men sinned'* (Rm 5:12). Adam's sin brought spiritual death to himself and to all his descendants: *'for in Adam all die'* (1Co 15:22). Sin, like some beast of prey, would henceforth stand at the door of every human heart as God warned Cain *'If you do well, will you not be accepted? And if you do not do well, sin is couching at the door; its desire is for you, but you must master it'* (Gn 4:7).

Figure 10: *The sacrifices of Cain and Abel*

It is however impossible to *'do well'* without God's grace:

> I find it to be a law that when I want to do right, evil
> lies close at hand. For I delight in the law of God, in

> my inmost self, but I see in my members another law
> at war with the law of my mind and making me
> captive to the law of sin which dwells in my
> members. Wretched man that I am! Who will deliver
> me from this body of death? Thanks be to God
> through Jesus Christ our Lord! So then, I, of myself,
> serve the law of God with my mind, but with my
> flesh I serve the law of sin (Rm 7:21–25).

To remedy this, God instituted means by which sins may
be forgiven. Central to forgiveness was the need for the
sinner to appear before a priest, God's representative, to
confess all wrongdoing, and to make the prescribed sin
offering. The various offences and their penalties can be
found in the Book of Leviticus, Chapters 4–7. The following,
however, is typical of what the sinner must do in order to
obtain forgiveness of his transgression.

> The Lord said to Moses, 'If anyone sins and commits
> a breach of faith against the Lord by deceiving his
> neighbour in a matter of deposit or security, or
> through robbery, or if he has oppressed his neigh-
> bour or has found what was lost and lied about it,
> swearing falsely — in any of all the things which men
> do and sin therein, when one has sinned and become
> guilty, he shall restore what he took by robbery, or
> what he got by oppression, or the deposit which was
> committed to him, or the lost thing which he found,
> or anything about which he has sworn falsely; he
> shall restore it in full, and shall add a fifth to it, and
> give it to him to whom it belongs, on the day of his
> guilt offering. And he shall bring to the priest his
> guilt offering to the Lord, a ram without blemish out
> of the flock, valued by you at the price for a guilt
> offering; and the priest shall make atonement for
> him before the Lord, and he shall be forgiven for any
> of the things which one may do and thereby become
> guilty' (Lv 6:1–7).

The transgressor was obliged first to make full restoration
of what he had unjustly taken; second, to compensate the
person he had injured and third, to appear before the priest

with the prescribed guilt offering. Since the priest was to value the guilt offering, it is obvious that the transgressor had to confess the nature of his sin, for *'who can say "I have made my heart clean; I am pure from my sin"?'* (Pr 2:9).

Confession

The confession of sins to a priest was a common practice in the Old Covenant and in Jewish religious life: *'He who conceals his transgressions will not prosper, but he who confesses and forsakes them will obtain mercy'* (Pr 28:13). When, therefore, John the Baptist appeared at the river Jordan *'there went out to him all the country of Judea, and all the people of Jerusalem; and they were baptised by him in the river Jordan, confessing their sins'* (Mk 1:5). It was natural that the people would confess to John since, as the son of Zechariah the priest, he was a priest. This practice, so necessary for the forgiveness of sins, is continued in the New Covenant as can be seen from St James' injunction, *'confess your sins to one another, and pray for one another, that you may be healed'* (Jm 5:16).

Through the sacraments of Christian initiation, Christians receive the new life of Christ but, nonetheless, they are subject to sin, suffering, illness, and death in this world. Further, this new life, even though *'hid with Christ in God'* (Col 3:3) can be weakened and even lost by sin. Christ, who forgave the sins of many, willed that His Church should continue His work of healing and salvation among her own members and so He instituted the two sacraments of healing: the sacrament of Penance and the sacrament of Anointing of the Sick.

Now, since the new life received in Christian initiation abolishes neither the frailty and weakness of human nature nor its inclination to sin, the Apostle warns

> If we say we have no sin, we deceive ourselves, and the truth is not in us. If we confess our sins, he is faithful and just, and will forgive our sins and cleanse us from all unrighteousness. If we say we

have not sinned, we make him a liar, and his word
is not in us (1Jn 1:8–10).

A sacrament, therefore, for the forgiveness of sins is necessary both for conversion and for the restoration and renewal
of the grace of Baptism. St Peter's restoration after he had
denied his Master three times testifies to this (Lk 22:61; Jn
21:15–17). Now the Father, undoubtedly, had sent His Son
to save sinners by pardoning their sins. The angel had
declared this much to St Joseph: '*you shall call his name Jesus,
for he will save his people from their sins*' (Mt 1:21). Christ said
it of Himself: '*For I came not to call the righteous, but sinners*'
(Mt 9:13), and St Paul confirmed it: '*Christ Jesus came into
the world to save sinners*' (1Tm 1:15). From the beginning of
His public life, Christ openly forgave sin, so much so, that
the scribes thought His plain declaration of doing so
blasphemous. A case in point is that of the paralytic carried
by his four friends to the Lord for healing:

> And they came, bringing to him a paralytic carried
> by four men. And when they could not get near him
> because of the crowd, they removed the roof above
> him; and when they had made an opening, they let
> down the pallet on which the paralytic lay. And
> when Jesus saw their faith, he said to the paralytic,
> 'My son, your sins are forgiven.' Now some of the
> scribes were sitting there, questioning in their hearts,
> 'Why does this man speak thus? It is blasphemy!
> Who can forgive sins but God alone?' And immedi-
> ately Jesus, perceiving in his spirit that they thus
> questioned within themselves, said to them, 'Why
> do you question thus in your hearts? Which is easier,
> to say to the paralytic, 'Your sins are forgiven,' or to
> say, 'Rise, take up your pallet and walk'? But that
> you may know that the Son of man has authority on
> earth to forgive sins' — he said to the paralytic — 'I
> say to you, rise, take up your pallet and go home.'
> And he rose, and immediately took up the pallet and
> went out before them all; so that they were all
> amazed and glorified God, saying, 'We never saw
> anything like this!' (Mk 2:3–12).

The miraculous restoration of the atrophied muscles of the paralytic is sufficient proof that Christ had, indeed, forgiven his sins.

Since Christ had the authority to forgive sins, He could delegate this authority to whosoever He wished. At Caesarea Philippi, He promised to do so (Mt 16:19; 18:18) and did, in fact, on the day of His Resurrection confer the power to forgive sins on St Peter and the Apostles (Jn 20:23). Specifically, when Christ entrusted the keys of the kingdom of heaven to Simon Peter, He gave him supreme jurisdiction over the whole Church and, this necessarily included the power to forgive sins because sin alone excludes one from the kingdom of heaven (Mt 16:18). He also promised the other Apostles this same power when He said, *'Truly, I say to you, whatever you bind on earth shall be bound in heaven, and whatever you loose on earth shall be loosed in heaven'* (Mt 18:18).

On the very day of His Resurrection, Christ fulfilled His promise when He, formally and explicitly, conferred the power of forgiving sins on His Apostles

> 'As the Father has sent me, even so I send you.' And when he had said this, he breathed on them, and said to them, 'Receive the Holy Spirit.' If you forgive the sins of any, they are forgiven; if you retain the sins of any, they are retained (Jn 20:21–23).

It is particularly striking that He should give this power to the very men who had denied and deserted Him in His greatest hour of need just two days previously.

In granting the discretionary power to forgive or to retain sins to His Apostles, Christ indicated that sins were to be pardoned only after a careful judgment of the penitent's disposition, from which it follows that the sins must be heard in order for a judgement to be made. Christ came to forgive sins and did so personally on many occasions. The Church, which He founded to carry out His mission until His return, likewise, must have that same power to forgive sins if she is to fulfil her mandate.

The Sacrament of Anointing of the Sick

Sickness and suffering, with the accompanying experiences of powerlessness, limitation, and finitude, have always been among the most serious challenges human beings face in life. In every illness, one catches a glimpse of death. In fact, the writings of the Old Testament, even link sickness to sin and evil: *'some were sick through their sinful ways, and because of their iniquities suffered affliction; they loathed any kind of food, and they drew near to the gates of death'* (Ps 106:17–18). God, however, in the face of human suffering, has revealed Himself as *'I am the Lord, your healer'* (Ex 15:26). In His mercy, He healed King Hezekiah who, after his recovery, recognised that faithfulness to God in observing His law restores life:

> Lo, it was for my welfare that I had great bitterness; but thou hast held back my life from the pit of destruction, for thou hast cast all my sins behind thy back. For Sheol cannot thank thee, death cannot praise thee; those who go down to the pit cannot hope for thy faithfulness. The living, the living, he thanks thee, as I do this day; the father makes known to the children thy faithfulness. The Lord will save me, and we will sing to stringed instruments all the days of our life, at the house of the Lord (Is 38:17–20).

The Christian understanding of human suffering is rooted in Isaiah's prophetic utterance regarding the Messiah whose bruises and grief would endow human suffering with a redemptive value that could be used to make reparation for the sins of others.

> Yet it was the will of the Lord to bruise him; he has put him to grief; when he makes himself an offering for sin, he shall see his offspring, he shall prolong his days; the will of the Lord shall prosper in his hand; he shall see the fruit of the travail of his soul and be satisfied; by his knowledge shall the righteous one, my servant, make many to be accounted

righteous; and he shall bear their iniquities (Is 53:10–11).

The Messiah's suffering will have an intercessory, reparative and redemptive value by which the sins of many will be pardoned.

> Therefore I will divide him a portion with the great, and he shall divide the spoil with the strong; because he poured out his soul to death, and was numbered with the transgressors; yet he bore the sin of many, and made intercession for the transgressors.' (Is 53:12).

The prophet also foresaw that God would usher in a time of healing, both physical and spiritual, for His people when all their offences would be pardoned and their illnesses healed.

> For the Lord is our judge, the Lord is our ruler, the Lord is our king; he will save us. ... Then prey and spoil in abundance will be divided; even the lame will take the prey. And no inhabitant will say, 'I am sick'; the people who dwell there will be forgiven their iniquity (Is 33:22–24).

Christ's compassion for the sick is at the heart of the Gospel motif. There are innumerable accounts of Him healing every kind of infirmity and sickness wherever He went:

> And he went about all Galilee, teaching in their synagogues and preaching the gospel of the kingdom and healing every disease and every infirmity among the people. So his fame spread throughout all Syria, and they brought him all the sick, those afflicted with various diseases and pains, demoniacs, epileptics, and paralytics, and he healed them (Mt 4:23–24).

These healing were also a resplendent sign that '*God has visited his people*' (Lk 7:16) and of the closeness of the Kingdom of God. Further, He used His clothing as a type of sacrament when He healed those who touched even its fringe.

> And when they got out of the boat, immediately the people recognized him, and ran about the whole neighbourhood and began to bring sick people on their pallets to any place where they heard he was. And wherever he came, in villages, cities, or country, they laid the sick in the market places, and besought him that they might touch even the fringe of his garment; and as many as touched it were made well (Mk 6:54–56).

Figure 11: *Christ heals the sick*

The Lord Jesus has the power not only to heal, but also to forgive sins and, since the sick need just such a Physician, He came to heal the whole person, body and soul. He frequently made use of signs when healing the sick: spittle (Mk 8:23) and the laying-on of hands (Lk 13:13), mud and washing (Jn 9:6). As the sick tried to touch him, *'for power came forth from him and healed them all'* (Lk 6:19) so also in the sacraments, Christ continues to 'touch' His people in order to heal them.

'What was spoken by the prophet Isaiah, "He took our infirmities and bore our diseases"' (Mt 8:17), was fulfilled by Christ personally and through His apostles whom He sent out to announce the presence of the kingdom of heaven, and who, as they went, *'cast out many demons, and anointed with oil many that were sick and healed them'* (Mk 6:13).

This is a prefiguration of the sacrament of the Anointing of the Sick, whereby those anointed have their sins forgiven and are freed from Satan's power. St James clearly indicated that the elders or priests of the Church have received the power to administer this sacrament to the sick:

> Is any among you sick? Let him call for the elders of the church, and let them pray over him, anointing him with oil in the name of the Lord; and the prayer of faith will save the sick man, and the Lord will raise him up; and if he has committed sins, he will be forgiven (Jm 5:14–15).

Hence, this sacrament has three effects. First, it gives the sick person the strength, peace and courage needed to overcome the difficulties that accompany serious illness or the frailty of old age. Further, not only is the sick person's trust and faith in God renewed but strength is also given to resist the temptation to discouragement and anguish in the face of death (Heb 2:15). This assistance from the Lord by the power of His Spirit is meant to lead the sick person to healing of the soul, as well as of the body, if such were God's will. Furthermore, the sick person's sins will be forgiven.

Second, since Christians have been consecrated to bear fruit, when sick, they will receive, from this sacrament, the grace and the strength to be united more closely to Christ in His Passion and so, participate in His redemptive work. *'I rejoice in my sufferings for your sake, and in my flesh I complete what is lacking in Christ's afflictions for the sake of his body, that is, the church'* (Col 1:24). Thus, just as Baptism began the process whereby the Christian is conformed to the death and Resurrection of Christ, so now the sacrament of the Anointing of the Sick completes it.

The third effect follows from this. The sacrament of the Anointing of the Sick enables a sick person to contribute spiritually to the sanctification of the Church and to the good of all for whom the Church herself suffers as she offers herself through Christ, her Head, to God the Father.

Thus, the sacrament of the Anointing of the Sick completes the holy anointings that mark the whole of Christian life, namely that of Baptism, which sealed the new life, and that of Confirmation, which strengthened the Christian for combat. This final anointing fortifies the end of the Christian's earthly life like a solid rampart for the final struggles before entering the Father's house.

The Sacrament of Holy Orders

Holy Orders is the sacrament of apostolic ministry through which the mission entrusted by Christ to His Apostles continues to be exercised in the Church until the end of time. Christ entrusted to the Apostles the office of teaching, sanctifying and governing in His name and by His power. When He founded the Church, He gave her His own authority and mission so that she could go out into the world to proclaim the Gospel and to act in His name. Consequently, no one, either as an individual or as a community, can validly give himself the mandate and the mission to proclaim the Gospel. A person sent by the Lord does not speak and act on his own authority, but by virtue of the Lord's authority. Nor does such a person receive his mandate from the community, but rather speaks to the community in the name of Christ. No one can bestow grace on himself; it must be offered, given and accepted. This fact presupposes the Apostles were ministers of grace, authorised and empowered by Christ from whom they receive the mission and faculty to act in His person as the Church's Head.

In His great high priestly prayer, Christ prayed for the fraternal unity of His Apostles whom He had chosen together (Lk 6:13) and sent out together. (Mk 16:20). He also included their successors in that prayer:

> I do not pray for these only, but also for those who believe in me through their word, that they may all be one; even as thou, Father, art in me, and I in thee, that they also may be in us, so that the world may believe that thou hast sent me (Jn 17:20–21).

Figure 12: *Christ washes St Peter's feet at the Last Supper*

The Apostles and their successors share in the triple office of Christ the Prophet, Priest and King through their own office of teaching, sanctifying and governing. They were formally inducted into their office when Christ, the High Priest of the New Law according to the order of Melchizedek (Ps 110:4; Heb 7:11), at the Last Supper instituted the Eucharistic Sacrifice, which He had just offered as a permanent and official act of worship. He ordained His Apostles as priests of the New Covenant, when, with the words *'Do this in remembrance of me'* (Lk 22:19), He commanded them to do as He had done. They could do as He commanded, only because He had given them the power to do what He had commanded, that is, to offer this self–same sacrifice as representatives and sharers in His Eternal Priesthood.

The Apostles, in turn, ordained men to the priesthood by the imposition of hands as St Paul reiterated to Timothy: *'Hence I remind you to rekindle the gift of God that is within you through the laying-on of my hands'* (2Tm 1:6). St Paul also charged Titus to appoint elders or priests: *'This is why I left you in Crete, that you might amend what was defective, and appoint elders in every town as I directed you'* (Tt 1:5). He, likewise, instructed the elders or priests at Ephesus to minister to the Church: *'Take heed to yourselves and to all the flock, in which the Holy Spirit has made you overseers, to care for the church of the Lord which he obtained with the blood of his own'* (Ac 20:28).

The Sacrament of Matrimony

Sacred Scripture opens with an account of the creation of man and woman in the image and likeness of God and concludes with a vision of *'the wedding-feast of the Lamb'* (Rev 19:9). God Himself, at the dawn of creation, instituted the matrimonial covenant by which a man and a woman establish between themselves a life-long partnership that, by its nature, is directed towards the good of the spouses and the procreation and education of their children. Christ elevated this matrimonial covenant to the dignity of a sacrament for the baptized so that the mutual love of husband and wife could mirror the absolute and unfailing love with which God loves the human race.

Created in the image and likeness of God who is Himself love, every human being has the fundamental and innate vocation to love. Since *'it is not good that the man should be alone'* (Gn 2:18) the woman, as 'flesh of his flesh', as his equal, and as his nearest in all things, is given to the man by God as a 'helpmate'. Thus, she represents God from whom all help comes (Ps 121:2). Although sin disrupted the harmonious communion between man and woman, marriage nonetheless remains a great blessing and source of joy for the human race. St John the Baptist referred to Christ as the bridegroom, saying, *'He who has the bride is the bridegroom; the friend of the bridegroom, who stands and hears him, rejoices greatly at the bridegroom's voice; therefore this joy of mine is now full'* (Jn 3:29).

Figure 13: *The Wedding Feast at Cana*

Christ, when asked why His disciples did not fast, referred to Himself as the Bridegroom, saying, '*Can the wedding guests mourn as long as the bridegroom is with them? The days will come, when the bridegroom is taken away from them, and then they will fast*' (Mt 9:15). Yet these affirmations were preceded by the most convincing affirmation of the great blessing of marriage, when, at His mother's request, Christ began His public life by performing His first miracle of changing water into wine during a wedding feast '*and his disciples believed in him*' (Jn 2:11).

In His preaching, Christ unequivocally declared the Creator's will and intention regarding the nuptial bond, that is, the matrimonial union of man and woman is indissoluble. Accordingly, when asked about the lawfulness of divorce, Christ reaffirmed the Creator's intention:

> Have you not read that he who made them from the beginning made them male and female, and said, 'For this reason a man shall leave his father and mother and be joined to his wife, and the two shall become one'? So they are no longer two but one. What therefore God has joined together, let not man put asunder (Mt 19:4–6).

As a result, not only did Christ restore marriage to its pristine condition of being an indissoluble bond between one man and one woman but He also made it a means of sanctification and a sign of His love for the Church He founded.

> For the husband is the head of the wife as Christ is the head of the church, his body, and is himself its Saviour... Christ loved the church and gave himself up for her, that he might sanctify her, having cleansed her by the washing of water with the word, that he might present the church to himself in splendour, without spot or wrinkle or any such thing, that she might be holy and without blemish.... This mystery is a profound one, and I am saying that it refers to Christ and the church (Ep 5:23–32).

Thus, the sacrament of Marriage becomes the vehicle whereby Christ enters into a couple's life to establish His domestic Church: *'For where two or three are gathered in my name, there am I in the midst of them'* (Mt 18:20). The entire Christian life bears the mark of the spousal love of Christ and the Church. Already Baptism, the entry into the Church, is a nuptial mystery. It is, so to speak, the nuptial bath, which precedes the wedding feast, that is, the Eucharist. Christian marriage, in its turn, becomes an efficacious sign, the sacrament of the covenant of Christ and the Church. Since it signifies and communicates grace, marriage between baptised persons is a true sacrament of the New Covenant.

Christ, out of His infinite love for humanity, instituted the seven sacraments as a remedy and a healing for the defects caused by sin. The sacraments confer sanctifying grace, which signifies a permanent supernatural attachment to God as well as freedom from grievous sin. *'But you were washed, you were sanctified, you were justified in the name of the Lord Jesus Christ and in the Spirit of our God'* (1Co 6:11). Baptism, Confirmation, and Eucharist are the sacraments of Christian initiation. They establish the common vocation of all Christ's disciples, a vocation to holiness and to evangelising the world. They confer the graces Christians need to live according to the Spirit during their life as pilgrims marching towards the heavenly homeland (Heb 12:22). The spiritual death caused by actual sin committed after Baptism is remedied by the sacrament of Confession, while the Anointing of the Sick enables the Christian to share in Christ's redemptive work. The last two sacraments, Holy Orders and Matrimony, are directed principally towards the salvation of others by conferring on the Christian receiving them a particular mission to build up the Church, as Christ's universal and domestic body respectively.

Apostolic governance

An integral part of every organisation is its governing body. Christ provided a governing body for His Church when He made His Apostles leaders with authority to supervise its activities. He warned them, however, that their governance was to be one of service, directed to the good of others: *'let the greatest among you become as the youngest, and the leader as one who serves. ... But I am among you as one who serves'* (Lk 22:26–27). Faithful and humble service is to be highly valued as St Paul wrote Timothy *'Let the elders who rule well be considered worthy of double honour, especially those who labour in preaching and teaching'* (1Tm 5:17). The Apostles also had the ultimate say in deciding disputes.

> If he refuses to listen to them, tell it to the church; and if he refuses to listen even to the church, let him be to you as a Gentile and a tax collector. Truly, I say to you, whatever you bind on earth shall be bound in heaven, and whatever you loose on earth shall be loosed in heaven (Mt 18:17–18).

Christ founded the Church that, through her, He *'might reconcile us ... to God in one body through the cross, thereby bringing the hostility to an end'* (Ep 2:16). Reconciliation with the Father comes by accepting Christ through the Church He founded. That is, by embracing the message of the Apostles, one accepts Christ and His Father who sent Him: *'He who receives you receives me, and he who receives me receives him who sent me'* (Mt 10:40). St Paul put it even more succinctly when he wrote,

> All this is from God, who through Christ reconciled us to himself and gave us the ministry of reconciliation; that is, in Christ God was reconciling the world to himself, not counting their trespasses against them, and entrusting to us the message of reconciliation. So we are ambassadors for Christ, God making his appeal through us. We beseech you on behalf of Christ, be reconciled to God (2Co 5:18–20).

Peter's primacy

In addition to a governing body, every organisation needs a head. Christ, therefore, covered this requirement by conferring, and later confirming, the primacy of Simon Peter over both his fellow Apostles and the Church.

The occasion for the conferral of the primacy took place at Caesarea Philippi, a remote area in the northern tip of Judea. In addition to being a place of pilgrimage for pagans, this site was considered one of the religious wonders of the ancient world. It had been used for animal and perhaps human sacrifice, and King Herod had built a temple to Caesar Augustus on top of the huge rock that still dominates the area. At the base of the rock was a deep, dark hole thought to be bottomless and known as the 'gates of hell.' It was before the pagan temple, before the gates of hell, before the place of blood sacrifice and ignorance that God the Father revealed Christ's divine nature to Simon Peter. Christ immediately acknowledged that this revelation was a truth beyond the grasp of the human intellect: *'Jesus answered him, "Blessed are you, Simon Bar-Jona! For flesh and blood has not revealed this to you, but my Father who is in heaven"'* (Mt 16:17). Using the symbol of the *'keys of the kingdom'*, He bestowed on Simon Peter the supreme authority over the Church.

> And I tell you, you are Peter, and on this rock I will build my church, and the gates of hell shall not prevail against it. I will give you the keys of the kingdom of heaven, and whatever you bind on earth shall be bound in heaven, and whatever you loose on earth shall be loosed in heaven (Mt 16:18–19).

The 'keys of the kingdom' refer to the power of access, the responsibility for the general care of the household and is a symbol of the power and authority that the steward of the kingdom exercised:

> In that day I will call my servant Eli'akim the son of Hilki'ah, and I will clothe him with your robe, and

> will bind your girdle on him, and will commit your
> authority to his hand; and he shall be a father to the
> inhabitants of Jerusalem and to the house of Judah.
> And I will place on his shoulder the key of the house
> of David; he shall open, and none shall shut; and he
> shall shut, and none shall open. And I will fasten
> him like a peg in a sure place, and he will become a
> throne of honour to his father's house (Is 22:20–23).

As the steward of the Davidic kingdom, Eli'akim was the
king's representative during the king's absence. Further,
among the Jewish people, the steward's office was succes-
sive and unchallenged and passed down either by father to
son or by appointment. In other words, although the
individual holding the office of steward would die, the
office itself would continue and would never diminish in
authority or in meaning. These prerogatives would naturally belong to Peter when Christ appointed him as steward
over His kingdom, the Church until He returned. It likewise
follows that since Christ established a Church with Peter as
head, then whenever Peter exercised his supreme authority
over the Church, his decision would be ratified in heaven.

On the night of His betrayal, Christ, quoting the prophet
Zechariah (13:7) told the Apostles that they would desert
Him: '*Jesus said to them, "You will all fall away; for it is written,
'I will strike the shepherd, and the sheep will be scattered'*" (Mk
14:27). Showing particular concern for Simon Peter, for
whom He had already prayed, Christ warned him of the
grave temptation he would face.

Specifically, Satan had been granted permission, as in
the case of Job (Jb 1:12;2:6) to test all the Apostles, but Christ
prayed for Peter in particular, not that he would not deny
but, that having denied, he would repent and build up the
faith of the other Apostles: '*Simon, Simon, behold, Satan
demanded to have you, that he might sift you like wheat, but I
have prayed for you that your faith may not fail; and when you
have turned again, strengthen your brethren*' (Lk 22:31–32).

After His Resurrection, Christ asked Simon Peter three
times whether he loved Him. In this way, He annulled

Simon Peter's triple denial and reconfirmed Peter's position as leader with full authority over both his fellow Apostles and the Church. He did this in the presence of the other Apostles so that there would be no dispute about Peter's leadership and authority.

> When they had finished breakfast, Jesus said to Simon Peter, 'Simon, son of John, do you love me more than these?' He said to him, 'Yes, Lord; you know that I love you.' He said to him, 'Feed my lambs.' A second time he said to him, 'Simon, son of John, do you love me?' He said to him, 'Yes, Lord; you know that I love you.' He said to him, 'Tend my sheep.' He said to him the third time, 'Simon, son of John, do you love me?' Peter was grieved because he said to him the third time, 'Do you love me?' And he said to him, 'Lord, you know everything; you know that I love you.' Jesus said to him, 'Feed my sheep' (Jn 21:15–17).

Simon Peter's pre-eminence is evident in the writings of the New Testament as he heads every list of the Apostles: '*The names of the twelve apostles are these: first, Simon, who is called Peter ...*' (Mt 10:2–4; Mk 3:14–19; Lk 6:13–16; Ac 1:13). Additionally, Simon Peter is mentioned by name 176 times in the New Testament, while the second most frequently named apostle is John at 46 times.

The birth of the Church

Christ founded a specific Church to continue His mission throughout the ages until the end of time. He promised not only to be with His Church: '*I am with you always, to the close of the age*' (Mt 28:20); but also that His Church would have the assistance and guidance of the Holy Spirit: '*I will pray the Father, and he will give you another Counsellor, to be with you for ever, even the Spirit of truth, whom the world cannot receive*' (Jn 14:16–17). The promise was fulfilled when the Holy Spirit descended on the Apostles at Pentecost and remained with them as they *'went forth and preached every-where, while the Lord worked with them and confirmed the message by the signs that attended it.'* (Mk 16:20) The closeness and importance of the connection between Christ's mission and that of His Church are well summarised in the Letter to the Hebrews. There, the faithful are reminded that, in these last days, God has spoken to them through His Son (Heb 1:1) and consequently, they should be scrupulous in their adherence to the apostolic teaching and witness since its veracity is vouched for both by God Himself with miracles and by the distribution of the gifts of the Holy Spirit:

> Therefore we must pay the closer attention to what we have heard, lest we drift away from it. For if the message declared by angels was valid and every transgression or disobedience received a just retri-bution, how shall we escape if we neglect such a great salvation? It was declared at first by the Lord, and it was attested to us by those who heard him, while God also bore witness by signs and wonders and various miracles and by gifts of the Holy Spirit distributed according to his own will (Heb 2:1–4).

The Acts of the Apostles record the events of Pentecost as well as the life of the Church in the years following. It is clear that the Acts is a historical document chronicling the establishment and initial functioning of the Church Christ founded. It was never intended to be a blueprint for building a church. The first two chapters record the birth of the Church; the next ten chapters document the activities of St Peter, in particular, his defence of the Church against the Jewish authorities, his ministering to the faithful, his organisation of the Church, his taking decisions and his acceptance of the Gentiles as members of the Church. The remaining fourteen chapters follow St Paul's missionary journeys as he brought the Gospel of Christ as well as the Church Christ founded to the Gentile world.

The birth of the Church is recorded in the first two chapters of the Acts of the Apostles and, in many ways, parallels the founding of the people of Israel at Sinai. Both events took place fifty days after Passover, with the twelve Apostles corresponding to the Twelve Tribes, and the descent of the Holy Spirit with the rush of a mighty wind and the appearance of tongues of fire paralleling the presence of God on the mountain amidst lightening and thunder. These are chronicled in Ac 2:1–2 and Ex 19:16–20; Dt 4:11–12. As the old covenant formed the people of Israel on Sinai, so the birth of the Church heralds in a *'new covenant, not in a written code but in the Spirit; for the written code kills, but the Spirit gives life'* (2Co 3:6). This comparison highlights the final contrast between the Upper Room and Mount Sinai, where three thousand believers received life in Jerusalem while three thousand apostates lost their lives at Sinai. *'And the sons of Levi did according to the word of Moses; and there fell of the people that day about three thousand men'* (Ex 32:28). Thus, in stark contrast, the justice of God was proclaimed by the letter of the Law, written in stone and delivered to Israel on Mount Sinai, while the mercy of God was announced by the spirit of the Law revealed in the Church, the new Israel, in the Upper Room in Jerusalem.

It was this new revelation with all its historical significance and prophetic fulfilment that St Peter authoritatively explained, on the day of Pentecost, to the assembled people, so that many believed. *'So those who received his* (St Peter's) *word were baptized, and there were added that day about three thousand souls. And they devoted themselves to the apostles' teaching and fellowship, to the breaking of bread and the prayers'* (Acts 2:41–42).

The three thousand people who were baptised immediately conformed themselves to the activities that are characteristic of the Church Christ founded, that is, the new Christians embraced the apostolic doctrine, devoted themselves to the community of the Church, partook of the Eucharist and persevered in prayer (Ac 2:42–43).

The Holy Spirit in the Church

In the years following that first Pentecost, despite opposition and persecution, the Church continued to grow '*So the churches were strengthened in the faith, and they increased in numbers daily*' (Acts 16:5). The presence and activity of the Holy Spirit was evident as He directed and governed the Church at first directly but, also indirectly through the visible authority of the Apostles. This somewhat parallels the experience of the people of Israel who were led and governed ordinarily by Moses: '*Thou didst lead thy people like a flock by the hand of Moses and Aaron*' (Ps 77:20); but in times of crisis, they had the benefit of direct divine intervention: '*Thou hast led in thy steadfast love the people whom thou hast redeemed, thou hast guided them by thy strength to thy holy abode*' (Ex 15:13).

On a number of occasions, the Holy Spirit intervened openly and directly in the Church to give instructions on what He wanted done. These direct interventions would invariably further the expansion and growth of the Church and her apostolate. The Spirit who said to Philip, the deacon, '*Go up and join this chariot*' (Ac 8:29) had initiated the conversion of the minister of Candace, the queen of Ethiopia. According to tradition, this minister was instrumental in the founding of what is now the Coptic Church in Ethiopia. Again, following instructions he had received from the Holy Spirit who said to him, '*Behold, three men are looking for you. Rise and go down, and accompany them without hesitation; for I have sent them*' (Ac 10:19–20), St Peter welcomed the Gentiles into the Church. When criticised by the circumcision party for admitting Cornelius and his household into the Church, St Peter defended his action saying he had merely obeyed the Spirit who had directed him: '*the Spirit told me to go with them, making no distinction. ... who was I that I could withstand God?*' (Ac 11:12–17). Similarly, the Spirit gave instructions to the elders of the Church in Antioch regarding Barnabas and Saul: '*While they were worshiping the Lord and fasting, the Holy Spirit said, "Set apart for me Barnabas and Saul for the work to which I have called them"'* (Ac 13:2). This, of course, initiated St Paul's universal mission to the Gentile world.

While the Holy Spirit did intervened directly on several occasions in the governance of the Church, ordinarily He would direct her affairs through the visible authority of the Apostles. When the issue of whether Gentiles were required to observe the law and customs of Moses arose, the Council of Jerusalem was summoned (Ac 15:1–6) and it authoritatively resolved the issue with the following decision:

> For it has seemed good to the Holy Spirit and to us to lay upon you no greater burden than these necessary things: that you abstain from what has been sacrificed to idols and from blood and from what is strangled and from unchastity (Ac 15:28–29).

Visibility of the Church

The Church Christ founded was certainly visible at Pentecost and has maintained a visible, continuous and cohesive presence throughout history. Its visibility can be established from the fact that it has always been an organisation that stood out plainly within the wider society as an organised body, consisting of teachers and those whom they taught, of leaders and followers who joined in public worship and made open profession of their beliefs. The Apostles admitted new members to the Church through the public rite of Baptism. They also made laws that affected the external behaviour of the faithful and they demanded that these laws be obeyed. They insisted that the faithful observe Christ's command to profess their faith openly: '*So every one who acknowledges me before men, I also will acknowledge before my Father who is in heaven*' (Mt 10:32).

Moreover, Christ, Himself, promised her not only His continuing and abiding presence '*I am with you always, to the close of the age*' (Mt 28:20) but also that no power would overwhelm her: '*And I tell you, you are Peter, and on this rock I will build my church, and the gates of hell shall not prevail against it*' (Mt 16:18).

Additionally, a type of the Church's visibility is that of the people of Israel who were visible throughout history and continue as an identifiable group to be visible right up to the present day, long after the promises made them had been fulfilled.

> For it is written that Abraham had two sons, one by a slave and one by a free woman. But the son of the slave was born according to the flesh, the son of the free woman through promise. Now this is an allegory: these women are two covenants. One is from Mount Sinai, bearing children for slavery; she is Hagar. Now Hagar is Mount Sinai in Arabia; she corresponds to the present Jerusalem, for she is in slavery with her children. But the Jerusalem above is free, and she is our mother. ... So, brethren, we are not children of the slave but of the free woman (Ga 4:22–31).

Indefectibility of the Church

Christ promised Simon Peter that the gates of hell, that is, death, destruction and the power of its enemies would not overcome the Church He would build (Mt 16:18). In making this unequivocal promise, Christ endowed His Church with the gift and seal of indefectibility, that is, His Church could never become defective in its constitution nor perish from the face of the earth. It was founded to last to the end of time, with its charism of teaching, governing and sanctifying its members intact.

In founding His Church as a visible society, Christ constituted the Apostles, whom He had told that '*the Spirit of your Father* (would be) *speaking through you*' (Mt 10:20), as its governing authority possessing the right to speak in God's name: '*Truly, truly, I say to you, he who receives any one whom I send receives me; and he who receives me receives him who sent me*' (Jn 13:20). To ensure that His Church would indeed be able to fulfil its mission, He promised, before His Passion, that it would have the uninterrupted and perpetual assistance of the Holy Spirit: '*I will pray the Father, and he will give you another Counsellor, to be with you for ever, even the Spirit of truth, whom the world cannot receive*' (Jn 14:16–17). At His Ascension, He comforted and reassured the Apostles with the promise of His own abiding presence and assistance (Mt 28:20).

A sign of contradiction

During His life on earth, Christ was a sign of contradiction and was opposed by the world. Even His own people rejected Him: '*He came to his own home, and his own people received him not*' (Jn 1:11). At His Presentation in the Temple, Simeon prophesied '*to Mary his mother, "Behold, this child is set for the fall and rising of many in Israel, and for a sign that is spoken against"*' (Lk 2:34). The opposition Christ faced during His public ministry sprang from the insincerity of the Pharisees, who condemned Him because of His association with sinners and tax collectors (Lk 5:30). Christ, however, exposed their hypocrisy by showing that they criticised both the asceticism of John the Baptist and His own affability:

> For John the Baptist has come eating no bread and drinking no wine; and you say, 'He has a demon'. The Son of man has come eating and drinking; and you say, 'Behold, a glutton and a drunkard, a friend of tax collectors and sinners!' Yet wisdom is justified by all her children (Lk 7:33–35).

Since the Church Christ founded is His Mystical Body, it should not be surprising that she, likewise, would experience the same opposition and contradiction. Indeed, He had even told His disciples to expect contradiction and opposition but always to remember that ultimately it was directed at Him.

If the world hates you, know that it has hated me before it hated you. If you were of the world, the world would love its own; but because you are not of the world, but I chose you out of the world, therefore the world hates you. Remember the word that I said to you, 'A servant is not greater than his master.' If they persecuted me, they will persecute you; if they kept my word, they will keep yours also. But all this they will do to you on my account, because they do not know him who sent me (Jn 15:18–21).

The term church

The word 'church' means a calling forth, as well as a council or an assembly. Whilst Christ founded one Church with a central authority, portions of it are also called Church. The persecution of the Church in Jerusalem (Ac 8:1), as well as the missionary activity of the disciples, led to the establishment of communities of believers in various places outside of Jerusalem. These communities are not only part of the one Church but also, are the one Church in a particular place. Thus, St Paul wrote to the Church in particular places: *'To the church of God which is at Corinth'* (2Co 1:1), *'to the Church of the Thessalonians in God the Father and the Lord Jesus Christ'* (1Th 1:1), and *'when this letter has been read among you, have it read also in the church of the Laodiceans'* (Col 4:16). He also wrote or referred to groups of churches in particular areas: *'To the churches of Galatia'* (Ga 1:2), *'the grace of God which has been shown in the churches of Macedonia'* (2Co 8:1), and *'I was still not known by sight to the churches of Christ in Judea'* (Ga 1:22). St Paul also referred to the private houses of the faithful as 'domestic' churches. Hence, he wrote: *'Greet Prisca and Aquila, … also all the churches of the Gentiles give thanks; greet also the church in their house'* (Rm 16:3–5); *'The churches of Asia send greetings. Aquila and Prisca, together with the church in their house, send you hearty greetings in the Lord,'* (1Co 16:19); *'To Philemon … and the church in your house'* (Philemon.1:2); and *'Nympha and the church in her house'* (Col 4:15). He also made reference to the Church according to its ethnic composition or geographical location. Thus, he said *'all the churches of the Gentiles give thanks'* (Rm 16:4), *'Churches of God in Christ Jesus which are in Judea'* (1Th 2:14), *'News of this came to the ears of the church in Jerusalem'* (Ac 11:22) and *'Now in the church at Antioch there were prophets and teachers ...'* (Ac 13:1). The Book of Revelation records the existence of the one Church in several cities: Ephesus (Rev 2:1), Smyrna (Rev 2:8), Pergamum (Rev 2:12), Thyatira (Rev 2:18), Sardis (Rev 3:1), Philadelphia (Rev 3:7), and Laodicea (Rev 3:14).

Points to Remember

a. *God loves His creation and sent His only Son, Jesus Christ, on a mission to redeem it.*

b. *Christ initiated His mission by preaching, teaching and sanctifying.*

c. *Christ entrusted to the twelve Apostles His own mission of preaching, teaching, redeeming and sanctifying the faithful until His return at the end of time.*

d. *The work of sanctification would be through the administration of the seven Sacraments, which are Baptism, Confirmation, Holy Eucharist, Confession, Anointing of the sick, Holy Orders and Matrimony.*

e. *Christ chose Simon Peter, in the presence of the other Apostles, to lead the apostolic band and He always showed a particular concern for him.*

f. *Having founded the Church on the Apostles, Christ promised them His abiding presence and the guidance of the Holy Spirit until His return at the end of time.*

g. *The Holy Spirit ordinarily directs the activities of the Church through the visible authority of the Apostles.*

h. *Despite the unremitting opposition and contradiction she faces and the imperfection of some of her members, the Church is indestructible because Christ promised that evil would never triumph over her and that He would remain with her until the end of time.*

i. *The Church manifests her presence in the world as a domestic institution, a local community and a universal society.*

6

Essential Characteristics of the Church Christ founded

Preamble

The world is confronted with a babel of Christian denominations all claiming to be the Church of Christ. Their doctrines are contradictory; and precisely in so far as any one of them regards its doctrines as fundamental, it declares those of its rival bodies to be false. In such a situation, it is impossible for the vast majority of human beings to distinguish the revelation of God from the inventions of man unless Christ endowed His Church with conspicuous characteristics that distinguish her from all other bodies. These characteristics would have to be such as would prove to a reasonable person that she and she alone is the Church that He founded. If she could not authenticate her claim, it would be impossible for her to warn anyone that to reject her is to reject Christ.

The Church Christ founded has specific characteristics by which she can be recognised. These characteristics or distinguishing marks are her oneness, her holiness, her catholicity and her apostolicity, otherwise expressed in the Nicene Creed as one, holy, catholic and apostolic Church. These characteristics are inseparably linked with each other and disclose certain essential features of the Church and her mission. She does not, however, possess these qualities of herself, but rather it is Christ who, through the Holy Spirit, makes His Church one, holy, catholic and apostolic, and it is He who calls her to manifest each of these qualities.

> Thus, it is only through faith that one is able to recognise
> that the Church's possession of these properties come
> from her divine source. Human reason, on the other
> hand, can clearly discern their historical manifestations.

Exposition

The Apostles' Creed was in use before AD 150 and professes
belief in 'the Catholic Church', that is, it declares that the
pre–eminent characteristic mark of the Church Christ
founded is its catholicity. Even today, Catholics, Orthodox
and most Protestants accept the Apostles' Creed and profess
belief in the Catholic Church. Interestingly, while the
smaller sects may not embrace the Apostles' Creed they,
nonetheless, instinctively recognise the characteristic of
universality as belonging to Christ's Church and, to appear
authentic, describe themselves as a worldwide church, an
international church or even a universal church.

When Christianity became a recognised religion in the
Roman Empire in AD 313, the persecution of the Church
ended but new teachers appeared teaching novel doctrines
about Christ. The most serious of these new teachings was
that of a priest called Arius who denied the divinity of
Christ. As successors of the Apostles, the bishops gathered
at Nicaea and taught authoritatively that Jesus Christ is
divine and has the same nature as God the Father. The
Apostles' Creed was then expanded to become the Nicene
Creed, which professes belief in 'one, holy, catholic and
apostolic Church'. The Council of Nicaea taught that unity,
apostolicity and holiness were also essential characteristics
of the Catholic Church.

Apostolicity is logically the first and most necessary
characteristic as it guarantees the one Church established
by Christ. Undoubtedly, the Church Christ founded must
be able to trace its roots back to the Apostles.

Unity and catholicity are necessarily linked and they both imply that the Church Christ founded is one and the same everywhere. Both unity and catholicity include time, stretching over the period from the Church's foundation until Christ's return and space extending over the entire face of the earth.

Holiness is an essential characteristic because the salvation of the human race is the Church's primary purpose. Holiness should be visible in her life, teaching and actions.

Points to Remember

a. *There is a multitude of Christian denominations all claiming to be Christ's Church. They are distinguished from each other by their own particular doctrines. In teaching any doctrine as fundamental, they automatically declare those of their rivals to be false and consequently that their rivals are not the Church Christ founded.*

b. *All Christian denominations accept that since Christ came for the salvation of the whole human race, membership to His Church is open to everyone and consequently this Church is necessarily catholic.*

c. *The Apostles' Creed, which was in use before AD 150 professes belief in 'the Catholic Church'.*

d. *The majority of Christians recognise the authority of the Council of Nicaea AD 325, which taught that unity, apostolicity, catholicity and holiness are essential characteristics of the Church Christ founded.*

e. *Through apostolicity, the Church can trace her roots back to the Apostles, and so to Christ.*

f. *Through her unity and catholicity, the Church remains the same over time and in all places.*

g. *The Church's primary mission is to make her members holy.*

7

The Church Christ founded is One

Preamble

The survival of any organisation depends on its members being in agreement with its essential nature and purpose, that is, what it is and what it does. Any disagreement about what it is or what it is supposed to do leads naturally into disunity, which in turn will bring about either the dissolution of the organisation or its mutation into something else. This does not mean that an organisation cannot grow or adapt to new circumstances or conditions but, rather, in growing and adapting, it must adhere to its original blueprint, that is, it must retain its original nature and founding purpose, if it is to remain the same organization.

The world is filled with many diverse Christian 'churches' claiming to be the authentic Church of Christ and it is obvious that where any two such churches disagree about a point of doctrine they cannot both be right, although they can both be wrong. Now, because of the large number of churches involved, it would be tedious and even unproductive to investigate the case of each individual claimant. A surer and more secure approach would be to establish the exact nature of the oneness and unity that Christ gave to His Church. Each claimant would then be able to measure their own case against this benchmark.

Christ established one Church on the twelve Apostles over whom Simon Peter had primacy. The Church was to preach the Gospel to all nations and bring them to unity of faith. After He had alerted His Apostles to the threats against unity, Christ consoled them with the assurance that the Spirit of truth would guide them to the complete truth. When pseudo-teachers appeared and tried to lead the faithful astray with their erroneous doctrines, the Apostles confronted them either by appealing to the faith that had been originally preached or by exercising their apostolic authority to call the dissenters to obedience. To preserve her essential nature and purpose, the Church Christ founded must maintain her oneness and unity by professing one faith, by offering one form of worship and by adhering to one universally-recognised form of government.

Exposition

1. Oneness of the Church

The prophet Isaiah's declaration that God is Israel's husband, '*For your Maker is your husband, the Lord of hosts is his name; and the Holy One of Israel is your Redeemer, the God of the whole earth he is called*' (Is 54:5), is echoed by St Paul in regard to Christ and the Church: '*I feel a divine jealousy for you, for I betrothed you to Christ to present you as a pure bride to her one husband*' (2Co 11:2).

There are many references in St Paul's letters to the Church as the body of Christ as well to Christ's Bride. In his letter to the Ephesians, however, St Paul joined these two concepts together within the context of the marriage covenant.

> Christ is the head of the church, his body, and is himself its Saviour… Christ loved the church and gave himself up for her, that he might sanctify her, having cleansed her by the washing of water with the word,

> that he might present the church to himself in splen-
> dour, without spot or wrinkle or any such thing, that
> she might be holy and without blemish (Ep 5:23–27).

He concluded his exposition by quoting Genesis '*For this reason a man shall leave his father and mother and be joined to his wife, and the two shall become one flesh*' (Gn 2:24), and summed up the nuptial doctrine saying '*This mystery is a profound one, and I am saying that it refers to Christ and the church*' (Ep 5:31–32).

The veil, however, is partially lifted from the mystery when it is recalled that

> If there is a physical body, there is also a spiritual
> body. ... But it is not the spiritual which is first but
> the physical, and then the spiritual. The first man
> was from the earth, a man of dust; the second man
> is from heaven. As was the man of dust, so are those
> who are of the dust; and as is the man of heaven, so
> are those who are of heaven. Just as we have borne
> the image of the man of dust, we shall also bear the
> image of the man of heaven (1Co 15:44, 46–49).

Thus, as Eve was the first man's 'flesh and bone' body and bride, so the Church is the second man's 'mystical' body and Bride.

Adam and Eve — Christ and His Church

The narrative of the first creation ends with God's creation of a man named Adam. 'Adam' is the name of an individual, the founding father of the human race and, is also the Hebrew word for 'humanity'. '*So God created man in his own image, in the image of God he created him; male and female he created them*' (Gn 1:27). That is, the image of God is found not only in the individual but also in the union of husband and wife.

Forming Adam's body from virgin earth, God '*breathed into his nostrils the breath of life; and man became a living being*' (Gn 2:7). Adam's disobedience, however, brought spiritual death to humanity. To restore humanity to life, God decreed that in the fullness of time '*a virgin shall conceive and bear a* son' (Is 7:14) who would *'save his people from their sins'* (Mt 1:21). This was the beginning of the second or new creation, which Isaiah foretold *'For as the new heavens and the new earth which I will make shall remain before me, says the Lord'* (Is 66:22). Christ referred to it when He declared Himself to be *'the resurrection and the life'* (Jn 11:25). St John, also, saw it in its fullness and perfection *'Then I saw a new heaven and a new earth; for the first heaven and the first earth had passed away, ... And he who sat upon the throne said, "Behold, I make all things new"'* (Rev 21:1,5).

In the renewal of all things, there is a certain parallel between the old and the new creations in as much *'as woman was made from man, so man is now born of woman'* (1Co 11:12). In particular, as the first Adam was formed from virgin earth, so the second Adam, uniting flesh to Himself, was conceived by the power of the Holy Spirit and born of the Virgin Mary.

Figure 14: *The Annunciation*

Another parallel is seen in the creation of Eve, Adam's bride, when *'the Lord God caused a deep sleep to fall upon the man, and while he slept took one of his ribs and closed up its place with flesh; and the rib which the Lord God had taken from the man he made into a woman'* (Gn 2:21-22). It was whilst the second Adam on the Cross slept in death that *'one of the soldiers pierced his side with a spear, and at once there came out blood and water'* (Jn 19:34) to reveal the Church, Christ's Bride. St John noted, *'This is he who came by water and blood, Jesus Christ, not with the water only but with the water and the blood'* (1Jn 5:6) to indicate that full membership to the Church, the body of Christ, is attained through Baptism (water) and the Eucharist (blood). The Divine breath provided the third parallel. God breathed into the nostrils of the first Adam that he might become a living being. Christ, the Son of God, on the day of His resurrection, breathed His life-giving Spirit on His Church, represented by His Apostles, that she might give and sustain the life of her members by forgiving them their sins: *'He breathed on them, and said to them, "Receive the Holy Spirit. If you forgive the sins of any, they are forgiven"'* (Jn 20:23).

St Paul summed this up, saying *'Thus it is written, 'The first man Adam became a living being'; the last Adam became a life–giving spirit'* (1Co 15:45). That is, a double heritage is now being offered to humanity. By nature, all human beings are in solidarity in the person of Adam—man, animal and earthly. The baptised, however, belong to Christ's body, the Church, which mysteriously forms itself around Christ who is Spirit, source of life and who comes from heaven. Christ, the second Adam, is the Head of the new creation, the Church, of which the Apostle was its most ardent promoter:

> From now on, therefore, we regard no one from a human point of view; even though we once regarded Christ from a human point of view, we regard him thus no longer. Therefore, if any one is in Christ, he is a new creation; the old has passed away, behold, the new has come (2Co 5:16–17).

Thus, as the first Adam had one bride, Eve, who by nature is *'the mother of all living'* (Gn 3:20), so the second Adam, Christ has only one Bride, the Church who is the mother of all who are reborn through water and the Holy Spirit and are now living supernatural lives.

One Church, many members

The first explicit mention of the Church in the Gospels is at Caesarea Philippi when Christ promised to build an indefectible Church: *'you are Peter, and on this rock I will build my church, and the gates of hell shall not prevail against it'* (Mt 16:18). It is clear from the Lord's words that His Church, His body, is one and not many. Further, since Christ died for the salvation of every human being, membership to His Church is open to the entire human race, which has to be gathered into one flock with one shepherd: *'And I have other sheep that are not of this fold; I must bring them also, and they will heed my voice. So there shall be one flock, one shepherd'* (Jn 10:16). With these words, Christ declared the missionary nature of His Church, namely that it should seek His sheep from among the nations. The Apostles then, by preaching the Gospel, would be the voice of Christ to the extent that anyone wilfully rejecting the Apostles' teaching automatically rejects Christ, and ultimately His Father: *'He who hears you hears me, and he who rejects you rejects me, and he who rejects me rejects him who sent me'* (Lk 10:16).

The Church's absolute oneness was foretold in the Song of Songs under the image of a dove: *'My dove, my perfect one, is only one, the darling of her mother, flawless to her that bore her'* (Sg 6:9) and is described in the Acts of the Apostles as *'the company of those who believed were of one heart and soul, and no one said that any of the things which he possessed was his own, but they had everything in common'* (Ac 4:32). The unity and brotherhood of Christ's Church are above all the embodiment on earth of the divine accord in heaven:

> I do not pray for these only, but also for those who
> believe in me through their word, that they may all

> be one; even as thou, Father, art in me, and I in thee,
> that they also may be in us, … that they may be one
> even as we are one, I in them and thou in me, that
> they may become perfectly one (Jn 17:21–23).

This prayer for unity is echoed by St Paul who saw the visible unity of the body of Christ as an external sign of the oneness of the Spirit who dwells within it. There is, he wrote, '*one body and one Spirit*' (Ep 4:4). As in any living organism, the union of the members in one body is the sign of a single animating principle within, so it is with the Church.

The human body comprises many members each functioning according to their nature to promote the good of the whole body. St Paul used this as an analogy to describe the relationship between Christ and His Church: '*For just as the body is one and has many members, and all the members of the body, though many, are one body, so it is with Christ*' (1Co 12:12). Through the sacrament of Baptism, Christ, who '*is the head of the body, the church*' (Col 1:18), enrols members from '*every tribe and tongue and people and nation*' (Rev 5:9) in His Church where they all enjoy a fundamental equality: '*For by one Spirit we were all baptized into one body—Jews or Greeks, slaves or free—and all were made to drink of one Spirit. For the body does not consist of one member but of many*' (1Co 12:13–14).

Within the human body, there are many members carrying out diverse functions and each member has its own indispensable task for maintaining the good of the whole body, which itself remains fundamentally one.

> And if the ear should say, 'Because I am not an eye,
> I do not belong to the body,' that would not make it
> any less a part of the body. If the whole body were
> an eye, where would be the hearing? If the whole
> body were an ear, where would be the sense of
> smell? But as it is, God arranged the organs in the
> body, each one of them, as he chose. If all were a
> single organ, where would the body be? As it is,
> there are many parts, yet one body (1Co 12:16–20).

The Church likewise, with its individual members, differently gifted, is one body and is also the very fullness of Christ Himself: '*He has put all things under his feet and has made him the head over all things for the church, which is his body, the fullness of him who fills all in all*' (Ep 1:22–23).

The initial social cohesion and community–sharing spirit enjoyed by the early Church was soon fractured by cultural differences and ethnic rivalry '*when the disciples were increasing in number, the Hellenists murmured against the Hebrews because their widows were neglected in the daily distribution*' (Ac 6:1). This problem was quickly resolved by the Apostles' prompt action in appointing seven deacons to take care of the material needs of the community, while they, the Apostles, devoted themselves to the more important task of preaching and teaching. '*And the twelve summoned the body of the disciples and said, "It is not right that we should give up preaching the word of God to serve tables"*' (Ac 6:2). Since the dispute between the Jewish and Gentile Christians was not doctrinal, its resolution was easily achieved so that '*the word of God increased; and the number of the disciples multiplied greatly in Jerusalem, and a great many of the priests were obedient to the faith*' (Ac 6:7). Thus, the institution of the diaconate helped to preserve the Church's unity, which consisted in an essential oneness in belief, teaching and practice: '*one Lord, one faith, one baptism, one God and Father of us all, who is above all and through all and in all*' (Ep 4:5).

2. Unity of the Church

To the accusation that He was possessed and was casting out demons by the power of Beelzebul, Christ responded with an example drawn from common experience:

> How can Satan cast out Satan? If a kingdom is divided against itself, that kingdom cannot stand. And if a house is divided against itself, that house will not be able to stand. And if Satan has risen up

against himself and is divided, he cannot stand, but
is coming to an end (Mk 3:23–26).

That is, no social entity, from the smallest household to the
largest city or kingdom, can survive for long without an
inherent unity. Unity, therefore, must be a primary characteristic of the Church Christ founded since He promised
that His Church would stand secure until His return at the
end of time.

Additionally, Christ was well aware that His Church's unity
would be attacked and so, before He suffered, He prayed to
His Father for its preservation (Jn 17); and His prayer was
granted since

The prayer of a righteous man has great power in its
effects. Elijah was a man of like nature with
ourselves and he prayed fervently that it might not
rain, and for three years and six months it did not
rain on the earth. Then he prayed again and the
heaven gave rain, and the earth brought forth its
fruit (Jm 5:16–18).

To guard against disunity in His Church, Christ made Simon
Peter the special object of His concern and the pivot of His
Church's unity. Thus, at the Last Supper He said to Simon
Peter, '*Simon, Simon, behold, Satan demanded to have you, that
he might sift you like wheat, but I have prayed for you that your
faith may not fail; and when you have turned again, strengthen
your brethren*' (Lk 22:31–32).

The sense of Christ's statement is that, as in the case of
Job, (Jb 1:12; 2:6) Satan had received permission to test the
Apostles' faith and even to set them at variance with each
other. Christ, however, had prayed for Simon specifically,
so that, even though, through lack of courage, he stumbled,
he would nonetheless be preserved from teaching error and
would always be the lynchpin of apostolic unity.

Later on that night, while walking with His disciples to
the Garden of Gethsemane, Christ prayed for the unity of
His Church down through the ages:

I do not pray for these only, but also for those who believe in me through their word, that they may all be one; even as thou, Father, art in me, and I in thee, that they also may be in us, so that the world may believe that thou hast sent me. ... that they may be one even as we are one, I in them and thou in me, that they may become perfectly one, so that the world may know that thou hast sent me and hast loved them even as thou hast loved me (Jn 17:20–23).

Figure 15: *Christ prays in the Garden of Gethsemane*

Undoubtedly, His prayer was both heard and answered since *'In the days of his flesh, Jesus offered up prayers and supplications, with loud cries and tears, to him who was able to save him from death, and he was heard for his godly fear'* (Heb 5:7).

Christ gave His apostles the mandate to make disciples of all nations, to baptize them and teach them to observe all that He had commanded (cf. Mt 28:19-20). This implies that persevering in the oneness and unity of His Church is only possible by adhering to His teaching and keeping His commandments.

The bonds of unity

Now it should be noted that unity does not exclude diversity. Consequently, the Church Christ founded, while being intrinsically one, possesses within itself a legitimate diversity arising from cultural influences, theological emphases and historical developments; and it could hardly be otherwise. Those who disagree with definitive Church teaching or wilfully separate themselves from legitimate Church authority merely abandon the unity of the Church Christ founded since, in the words of St Paul, *'no other foundation can anyone lay than that which is laid, which is Jesus Christ'* (1Co 3:11). The Church Christ founded also has an inherent unity that is preserved by charity, which *'binds everything together in perfect harmony'* (Col 3:14).

The nature of the bonds of the Church's unity on earth was evident from the day of Pentecost when the disciples *'devoted themselves to the apostles' teaching and fellowship, to the breaking of bread and the prayers'* (Ac 2:42). The first bond consists in a unity in belief; that is, a profession of the one Faith, received from the Apostles. The second bond is unity of Sacraments; that is, a common celebration of the means of grace, of divine worship and especially of the Eucharist or the *'breaking of bread'*. The third bond is unity of Ecclesiastical Governance; that is, the maintenance of the fellowship of the Apostles through obedience to the divinely established authority, by which the fraternal concord of God's family is assured. *'Obey your leaders and submit to them; for they are keeping watch over your souls, as men who will have to give account. Let them do this joyfully, and not sadly, for that would be of no advantage to you'* (Heb 13:17). The Church's bonds of unity are neatly summarised by St Paul who declared *'There is one body and one Spirit, just as you were called to the one hope that belongs to your call, one Lord, one faith, one baptism, one God and Father of us all, who is above all and through all and in all'* (Ep 4:4–6).

3. Enemies of unity

History is replete with cases of opportunists who, even to the extent of destroying fraternal unity, eagerly take advantage of a situation from which they can benefit personally. For example, when Abram left Ur, his nephew Lot went with him and naturally shared in his uncle's prosperity. In due time, *'the land could not support both of them dwelling together; for their possessions were so great that they could not dwell together, and there was strife between the herdsmen of Abram's cattle and the herdsmen of Lot's cattle'* (Gn 13:6–7). Abram, to avoid a full scale family feud, suggested that they separate and he even gave Lot the choice of where to go. *'Abram said to Lot, "Let there be no strife between you and me, and between your herdsmen and my herdsmen; for we are kinsmen. Is not the whole land before you? Separate yourself from me. If you take the left hand, then I will go to the right; or if you take the right hand, then I will go to the left"'* (Gn 13:8–9). Looking only to his own advantage and seeing *'that the Jordan valley was well watered everywhere like the garden of the Lord, like the land of Egypt … Lot chose for himself all the Jordan valley, and Lot journeyed east'* (Gn 13:10–11); and he separated himself from his uncle.

While Lot shattered unity for material advantage, others do so for personal aggrandisement, as is illustrated by the case of some exorcists, who made use of the power of Christ's name without, however, making any effort to become disciples. This caused the Apostle John to complain to the Lord

> 'Master, we saw a man casting out demons in your
> name, and we forbade him, because he does not

follow with us.' But Jesus said to him, 'Do not forbid him; for he that is not against you is for you' (Lk 9:49–50).

Christ's response was not a blanket approval for those who operate unilaterally, but rather one of tolerance, as in the case where the good seed and the bad are allowed to grow together. At harvest time, He is able to separate the weeds from the good crop (Mt 13:24-30). In a similar manner, He would take care of those who, by wilfully rejecting the apostolic authority, reject His own divine authority:

> Not every one who says to me, 'Lord, Lord,' shall enter the kingdom of heaven, but he who does the will of my Father who is in heaven. On that day many will say to me, 'Lord, Lord, did we not prophesy in your name, and cast out demons in your name, and do many mighty works in your name?' And then will I declare to them, 'I never knew you; depart from me, you evildoers' (Mt 7:21–23).

Whilst those acting outside of the parameters of the established authority rupture their unity with the Church, those who contradict the Church's authoritative teaching do more serious damage. The former is a schismatic act breaking the bonds of love and obedience; the latter is heretical and actually corrupts the truth revealed by God.

Christ said of Satan that

> he was a murderer from the beginning, and has nothing to do with the truth, because there is no truth in him. When he lies, he speaks according to his own nature, for he is a liar and the father of lies (Jn 8:44).

The principle strategy used by *'that ancient serpent, who is called the Devil and Satan, the deceiver of the whole world'* (Rev 12:9) to seduce and alienate human beings from God is the creation of doubt, followed by outright contradiction and ending in deception and a travesty of the truth. Those unwilling to accept the Church's teachings were warned by St Paul that *'the Spirit expressly says that in later times some will depart from the faith by giving heed to deceitful spirits and doctrines of demons'* (1Tm 4:1). To counter this diabolical deception, St John wrote emphatically, *'Beloved, do not believe every spirit, but test the spirits to see whether they are of God; for many false prophets have gone out into the world'* (1Jn 4:1).

False teachers

Since behaviour follows belief, the opinions of false teachers are always accompanied by grave spiritual dangers. At the beginning of His missionary life, Christ described the appearance and intentions of the promoters of false doctrine when He warned His disciples to *'Beware of false prophets, who come to you in sheep's clothing but inwardly are ravenous wolves'* (Mt 7:15). Towards the end of His missionary life, He again warned, *'And many false prophets will arise and lead many astray. And because wickedness is multiplied, most men's love will grow cold'* (Mt 24:11–12), meaning that since a *'sound tree cannot bear evil fruit, nor can a bad tree bear good fruit'* (Mt 7:18) erroneous teaching will eventually lead to corrupt morals. Therefore, to protect against this danger, He not only established a legitimate authority to speak in His name but also, warned His disciples to *'take heed that you are not led astray; for many will come in my name, saying, 'I am he' and, 'The time is at hand' Do not go after them'* (Lk 21:8). His warning indicates that imposters would impersonate Him, or claim to have some message from Him or some special insight into the true meaning of the Scriptures. In any case, they would contradict the apostolic teaching. This, undoubtedly, was what St Paul faced when he warned the Romans:

> I appeal to you, brethren, to take note of those who create dissensions and difficulties, in opposition to the doctrine which you have been taught; avoid them. For such persons do not serve our Lord Christ, but their own appetites, and by fair and flattering words they deceive the hearts of the simple–minded (Rm 16:17–18).

The doctrine referred to is, of course, the teachings the Apostles received directly from Christ and which they in turn faithfully passed on. Initially it consisted of the Apostles' oral teaching since they were still alive but later, it would include the teachings they committed to writing in the Gospels and the epistles. Because false teachers were causing divisions and confusion in the community with their own erroneous opinions, St Paul exhorted the Corinthians to adhere to the decisions of the Church's legitimate authority in order both to avoid deception and to maintain their ecclesial unity. '*I appeal to you, brethren, by the name of our Lord Jesus Christ, that all of you agree and that there be no dissensions among you, but that you be united in the same mind and the same judgment*' (1Co 1:10).

Then, because the Corinthians continued to maintain their confidence in dissenters who contradicted the official and authoritative teaching of the Church, St Paul, unlike the hireling who '*sees the wolf coming and leaves the sheep and flees*' (Jn 10:12), took action and castigated them for their gullibility:

> For if some one comes and preaches another Jesus than the one we preached, or if you receive a different spirit from the one you received, or if you accept a different gospel from the one you accepted, you submit to it readily enough.. (2Co 11:4).

He then went on stridently to denounce these '*peddlers of God's word*' (2Co 2:17) as '*false apostles, deceitful workmen, disguising themselves as apostles of Christ. And no wonder, for even Satan disguises himself as an angel of light. So it is not strange if his servants also disguise themselves as servants of righteousness*' (2Co 11:13).

To the Galatians who had been seduced by false teachers, he bluntly wrote that no creature, whether human nor angelic, had the authority to modify the Gospel initially preached to them.

> ... there are some who trouble you and want to pervert the gospel of Christ. But even if we, or an

angel from heaven, should preach to you a gospel contrary to that which we preached to you, let him be accursed. As we have said before, so now I say again, If any one is preaching to you a gospel contrary to that which you received, let him be accursed (Ga 1:8–9).

He also took precautionary measures to protect the integrity of the faith in the places where he had preached. For example, he left Timothy at Ephesus to ensure the continuance of the teaching of sound doctrine:

As I urged you when I was going to Macedonia, remain at Ephesus that you may charge certain persons not to teach any different doctrine, nor to occupy themselves with myths and endless genealogies which promote speculations rather than the divine training that is in faith; whereas the aim of our charge is love that issues from a pure heart and a good conscience and sincere faith. Certain persons by swerving from these have wandered away into vain discussion, desiring to be teachers of the law, without understanding either what they are saying or the things about which they make assertions (1Tm 1:3–7).

In contrast, he praised the Thessalonians for their honest and complete acceptance of and fidelity to the Gospel that had been preached to them.

And we also thank God constantly for this, that when you received the word of God which you heard from us, you accepted it not as the word of men but as what it really is, the word of God, which is at work in you believers (1Th 2:13).

The integrity of the faith and the salvation of the faithful are intricately intertwined and were so much at the heart of St Paul's missionary concern that he wrote to the Thessalonians encouraging them to remain faithful to both the spoken and the written word. '*So then, brethren, stand firm and hold to the traditions which you were taught by us, either by word of mouth or by letter'* (2Th 2:15). He concluded his letter with an admonition that *'If any one refuses to obey what we say in this letter, note that man, and have nothing to do with him, that he may be ashamed'* (2Th 3:14).

Deceivers

The chief weapon in Satan's armoury is deception, which he used very effectively in the Garden of Eden. *'The Lord God said to the woman, "What is this that you have done?" The woman said, "The serpent beguiled me, and I ate"'* (Gn 3:4). In this context, the Apostles were always *'afraid that as the serpent deceived Eve by his cunning,'* false apostles would lead the faithful *'astray from a sincere and pure devotion to Christ'* (2Co 11:3). Consequently, St John, to protect the faithful from the very real danger of deception arising from the persuasive arguments presented by false apostles, forbade them from having any contact (even including the ordinary and customary social greetings) with anyone who did not accept the apostolic teaching in its entirety: *'If anyone comes to you and does not bring this doctrine, do not receive him into the house or give him any greeting; for he who greets him shares his wicked work'* (2Jn 1:10–11).

St Jude was equally vigilant and openly exposed the deceivers, outlined their stratagems and denounced their surreptitious entry into the Church: *'For admission has been secretly gained by some who long ago were designated for this condemnation, ungodly persons who pervert the grace of our God into licentiousness and deny our only Master and Lord, Jesus Christ'* (Jude 4). He then went on to highlight their principal attribute, which was their rejection of the apostolic authority: *'Yet in like manner these men in their dreamings defile the flesh, reject authority, and revile the glorious ones'* (Jude 8.). He then zeroed in on their spiritual ancestry and the fate in store for them: *'Woe to them! For they walk in the way of Cain, and abandon themselves for the sake of gain to Balaam's error, and perish in Korah's rebellion'* (Jude 11).

The Apostle further noted that, like Balaam, they are motivated by financial considerations and, with bullying and flattery, provoked dissensions and division in order to gain control over the community.

> These are grumblers, malcontents, following their own passions, loud–mouthed boasters, flattering people to gain advantage. But you must remember, beloved, the predictions of the apostles of our Lord Jesus Christ; they said to you, 'In the last time there will be scoffers, following their own ungodly passions.' It is these who set up divisions, worldly people, devoid of the Spirit (Jude 16–19).

Rebels and dissenters

From the Mosaic Law, the twelve tribes of Israel received a common heritage; from the Davidic throne, they received a bond of unity together with an automatic share in the promises God had made to David. However, the misrule of Rehoboam, David's grandson, drove ten of the tribes into rebellion.

> And when all Israel saw that the king did not hearken to them, the people answered the king, 'What portion have we in David? We have no inheritance in the son of Jesse. Each of you to your tents, O Israel! Look now to your own house, David.' So all Israel departed to their tents. But Rehoboam reigned over the people of Israel who dwelt in the cities of Judah (2Ch 10:16–17).

Even though their cause had merit, these ten tribes, because of their rejection of the Davidic authority, actually lost out and they eventually disappeared as a distinct, identifiable people. Now since '*it is impossible that God should prove false*' (Heb 6:18), His promise to David (2S 7:11–16) remained true, valid and definite and eventually it was fulfilled in Jesus Christ, a descendant of David, of the tribe of Judah, (Lk 2:4) as St Paul declared in the synagogue of Antioch of Pisidia:

> God 'raised up David to be their king; of whom he
> testified and said, 'I have found in David the son of
> Jesse a man after my heart, who will do all my will.'
> Of this man's posterity God has brought to Israel a
> Saviour, Jesus, as he promised' (Ac 13:22–13).

History is not a series of random events or a catalogue of
coincidences, but rather the unfolding of a definite plan
*'according to the purpose of him who accomplishes all things
according to the counsel of his will'* (Ep 1:11). Thus God, the
Lord of creation, both respects the autonomy of His creatures and embraces their free acts to direct all things to their
proper end, which is the fulfilment of His will:

> For as the rain and the snow come down from
> heaven, and return not thither but water the earth,
> making it bring forth and sprout, giving seed to the
> sower and bread to the eater, so shall my word be
> that goes forth from my mouth; it shall not return to
> me empty, but it shall accomplish that which I
> purpose, and prosper in the thing for which I sent it
> (Is 55:10–12).

In order that the Church might realise her mission and
achieve the end for which Christ established her, that is the
salvation of souls, God bestows gifts and offices on certain
individuals who are to use them to build up the Church
Christ founded. In fact, according to St Paul, the Holy Spirit
distributes these gifts as He wills:

> All these are inspired by one and the same Spirit,
> who apportions to each one individually as he wills.
> For just as the body is one and has many members,
> and all the members of the body, though many, are
> one body, so it is with Christ (1Co 12:11–12).

Further, since the Holy Spirit is Himself the Church's source
of unity, these gifts can never be divisive as long as the
Church's members are all *'eager to maintain the unity of the
Spirit in the bond of peace. There is one body and one Spirit, just
as you were called to the one hope that belongs to your call'* (Ep
4:3–4).

However, even from apostolic times, there were certain people who, refusing *'to maintain the unity of the Spirit,'* (Ep 4:3) departed from the community of the Church. St John inferred from their departure that *'They went out from us, but they were not of us; for if they had been of us, they would have continued with us; but they went out, that it might be plain that they all are not of us'* (1Jn 2:19).

While these dissenters openly rejected the apostolic authority by their departure, others remained but engaged in denigration and used partisan politics to usurp the legitimate exercise of that authority:

> Diotrephes, who likes to put himself first, does not acknowledge my authority. So if I come, I will bring up what he is doing, prating against me with evil words. And not content with that, he refuses himself to welcome the brethren, and also stops those who want to welcome them and puts them out of the church (3Jn 9–11).

In addition to those who openly resisted the Apostles' authority, there were other people presumptuous enough to offer their own personal interpretation of Scripture as the authentic one. St Peter, however, made it very clear to them that *'First of all you must understand this, that no prophecy of scripture is a matter of one's own interpretation, because no prophecy ever came by the impulse of man, but men moved by the Holy Spirit spoke from God'* (2P 1:20–21). And regarding the writings of St Paul which were being privately reinterpreted, he warned

> So also our beloved brother Paul wrote to you according to the wisdom given him, speaking of this as he does in all his letters. There are some things in them hard to understand, which the ignorant and unstable twist to their own destruction, as they do the other scriptures (2P 3:15–16).

The authentic interpretation of Scripture, then, is the prerogative of the Church. Those, therefore, who have received the mandate to teach all nations everything that

Christ has commanded (Mt 28:20) articulate that true meaning faithfully since the Holy Spirit enlightens them as He enlightened the prophets before them (Jn 14:26).

In some cases, an immoral lifestyle or *'the love of money which is the root of all evils'* (1Tm 6:10) was the underlying motivation for rejecting apostolic authority as St Peter noted:

> There will be false teachers among you, who will secretly bring in destructive heresies … And many will follow their licentiousness, and because of them the way of truth will be reviled. And in their greed they will exploit you with false words (2P 2:1–3).

St Paul echoed St Peter's view when he denounced these false teachers as *'peddlers of God's word'* (2Co 2:17) who not only taught without apostolic mandate but also, taking advantage of the gullibility of the 'faithful', lined their pockets. *'For there are many insubordinate men, empty talkers and deceivers, especially the circumcision party; they must be silenced, since they are upsetting whole families by teaching for base gain what they have no right to teach'* (Tt 1:10–11).

St Paul was also conscious that the propagators of erroneous doctrines were frequently driven by pride and that, in addition to unsettling the faithful, they generated discord in the community. So while urging Timothy to teach sound doctrine, St Paul exposed the attitude and wiles of those who would oppose and undermine it.

> If any one teaches otherwise and does not agree with the sound words of our Lord Jesus Christ and the teaching which accords with godliness, he is puffed up with conceit, he knows nothing; he has a morbid craving for controversy and for disputes about words, which produce envy, dissension, slander, base suspicions, and wrangling among men who are depraved in mind and bereft of the truth, imagining that godliness is a means of gain (1Tm 6:3–5).

Then to mitigate the damage that erroneous doctrines were wrecking on the faithful, St Paul wrote to Timothy again, urging him to *'preach the word, be urgent in season and out of season, convince, rebuke, and exhort, be unfailing in patience and in teaching'* (2Tm 4:2).

False teachers, erroneous doctrines and the usurping of legitimate authority are dangerous enemies to the oneness and unity of the Church Christ founded, and they invariably lead to divisions and to the appearance of cults and sects.

4. Proliferation of sects

In the parable of the cockles (Mt 13:24–30, 36–43), Christ warned that Satan is always on the prowl and that he frequently uses human pride, weakness, avarice or other sins to instigate rebellion against all divinely established order.

Thus, even though God used to speak to Moses *'face to face, as a man speaks to his friend'* (Ex 33:11), this did not deter Moses' own brother and sister from challenging his authority: *'Miriam and Aaron spoke against Moses ... and they said, "Has the Lord indeed spoken only through Moses? Has he not spoken through us also?"'* (Num 12:1–2). Later, Korah, rashly claiming to be as holy and as divinely inspired as Moses, rebelled and led many people, including prominent men, astray and to destruction with him:

> Now Korah ..., and Dathan and Abiram ... took men; and they rose up before Moses, with a number of the people of Israel ... well–known men; and they assembled themselves together against Moses and against Aaron, and said to them, 'You have gone too far! For all the congregation are holy, every one of them, and the Lord is among them; why then do you exalt yourselves above the assembly of the Lord?' ... And as he finished speaking all these words, the ground under them split asunder; and the earth opened its mouth and swallowed them up, with their households and all the men that belonged to Korah and all their goods. So they and all that

belonged to them went down alive into Sheol (Num 16:1–3, 31–33).

The refusal to accept the truth that ordinarily God speaks through His chosen leaders who, more often than not, are less than perfect frequently leads to rebellion and to the establishment of a parallel governing system. God established David and his lineage as rulers over the kingdom of Israel: '… *your house and your kingdom shall be made sure for ever before me; your throne shall be established for ever*' (2S 7:16), but the foolishness and arrogance of Rehoboam, David's grandson, drove the people to rebellion and led to the division of the kingdom:

> When all Israel saw that the king did not hearken to them, the people answered the king, 'What portion have we in David? We have no inheritance in the son of Jesse. To your tents, O Israel! Look now to your own house, David.' So Israel departed to their tents. … So Israel has been in rebellion against the house of David to this day. And when all Israel heard that Jeroboam had returned, they sent and called him to the assembly and made him king over all Israel. There was none that followed the house of David, but the tribe of Judah only (1K 12:16, 19–20).

The revolt of the ten tribes resulted in the setting up of the kingdom of Israel in the north under Jeroboam while in the south Rehoboam continued to rule over Judah and Benjamin. To consolidate his rebellion, Jeroboam set up his own religion, with its own temple in rivalry with that of Jerusalem, with priests to compete with the Levites and with a form of worship at variance with that revealed to Moses:

> So the king took counsel, and made two calves of gold. And he said to the people, 'You have gone up to Jerusalem long enough. Behold your gods, O Israel, who brought you up out of the land of Egypt.' And he set one in Bethel, and the other he put in Dan. And this thing became a sin, for the people went to the one at Bethel and to the other as far as Dan. He also made houses on high places, and

> appointed priests from among all the people, who
> were not of the Levites. And Jeroboam appointed a
> feast on the fifteenth day of the eighth month like
> the feast that was in Judah, and he offered sacrifices
> upon the altar; so he did in Bethel, sacrificing to the
> calves that he had made. And he placed in Bethel
> the priests of the high places that he had made (1K
> 12:28–32).

Thus, in setting up a rebel authority even for apparently justifiable reasons and by instituting a false feast at a false shrine, ministered by false priests, before false gods, Jeroboam led the people into a false religion, false worship and to eventual ruin with the destruction of the kingdom of Israel by the Assyrians, as the prophet Hosea warned:

> To me they cry, My God, we Israel know thee. Israel
> has spurned the good; the enemy shall pursue him.
> They made kings, but not through me. They set up
> princes, but without my knowledge. With their
> silver and gold they made idols for their own
> destruction. …. Israel is swallowed up; already they
> are among the nations as a useless vessel. For they
> have gone up to Assyria, a wild ass wandering alone
> (Ho 8:2–4,8–9).

However, God's promise to David remained intact and was fulfilled in due course.

> Brethren, I may say to you confidently of the patriarch David that he both died and was buried, and
> his tomb is with us to this day. Being therefore a
> prophet, and knowing that God had sworn with an
> oath to him that he would set one of his descendants
> upon his throne, he foresaw and spoke of the resurrection of the Christ, that he was not abandoned to
> Hades, nor did his flesh see corruption. This Jesus
> God raised up, and of that we all are witnesses (Ac
> 2:29–32).

Throughout his letters, St Paul expressed his concern for the contemporary and future attacks that would be made on the teaching authority of the Church. He often referred to the fact that there would always be corrupters of the Gospel message who would set traps into which those who are not sufficiently vigilant would fall. However, despite his forewarnings, many people succumbed to the wiles of the false teachers. St Paul, however, had clearly indicated that their fall was a consequence of their lack of discernment, their gullibility and, since belief and behaviour are like the two faces of the same coin, their readiness to accept opinions that suited their immoral lifestyles: '*As Jannes and Jambres opposed Moses, so these men also oppose the truth, men of corrupt mind and counterfeit faith*' are able to capture those '*burdened with sins and swayed by various impulses, who will listen to anybody and can never arrive at a knowledge of the truth*' (2Tm 3:6–8).

St Paul's warning is timelessly valid, for despite the Lord's forewarning about false teachers and notwithstanding the vigilance of the Apostles, numerous sects with their various heresies did, and still do, appear and they continue to deceive many. Even though some dissensions, like Jeroboam's, may originate in an objective injustice, the censure pronounced by St Paul in his letter to the Romans is nonetheless applicable. '*I bear them witness that they have a zeal for God, but it is not enlightened. For, being ignorant of the righteousness that comes from God, and seeking to establish their own, they did not submit to God's righteousness*' (Rm 10:2–3).

Sadly, over the centuries, the number of dissenters would not only increase but the divergence from the apostolic teaching would grow ever wider and more speculative as St Paul had foreseen when he wrote St Timothy. '*I urged you … remain at Ephesus that you may charge certain persons not to teach any different doctrine, nor to occupy themselves with myths and endless genealogies which promote speculations rather than the divine training that is in faith*' (1Tm 1:3–4).

Points to Remember

a. *An organisation can only maintain its unity and identity as long as its members all embrace its essential nature, agree with its purpose and recognise the authority of its leader or head.*

b. *God created Adam; Adam being the name of an individual as well as the Hebrew name for humanity. With Eve as his 'flesh and bone' body and bride, Adam is the father and head of humanity.*

c. *To repair the damage done by Adam's sin, Christ, the Son of God, joined Himself to humanity by His birth from a virgin mother. With the Church as His 'mystical' body and Bride, Christ is the head of the redeemed humanity.*

d. *Christ founded one Church that would embrace all nations.*

e. *This Church has an inherent unity, which she derives from what she teaches by divine mandate.*

f. *The unity of the Church Christ founded is manifested in the profession of one faith received from the Apostles, in a common celebration of divine worship and in the maintenance of bonds of fellowship through obedience to the divinely established authority.*

g. *The Church's unity is threatened by disputes about what is to be believed, by setting up false forms of worship or by rejecting or refusing obedience to its legitimately established authority.*

h. *The Church Christ founded can never lose her inherent unity and those who reject her teaching or her authority merely separate themselves from her.*

8

The Church Christ founded is Holy

Preamble

Adam's sin introduced a radical discord in human nature so that holiness or sanctity is no longer found naturally in any human being or human institution. God, however, calls all human beings to holiness and He sent His Only-begotten Son to call sinners to repentance. To achieve this end, Christ founded a Church that would embrace sinners and would make them holy, that is, free them from sin and transform them into saints. Being Himself the source of all holiness, Christ as head, makes His body, the Church, holy through the doctrines, sacraments and morality she offers to her members. Thus, even if not all her members are holy, the Church herself is holy because she is the body of Christ.

Exposition

Adam's sin alienated the entire human race from God and brought about the spiritual death of all his descendants: '*sin came into the world through one man and death through sin, and so death spread to all men because all men sinned*' (Rm 5:12). Now, since the return to God is beyond natural human ability, God sent His Son to undo Adam's sin, to reconcile the human race to Himself, to restore human beings to the fullness of life (Jn 10:10) and to make them holy:

> Then as one man's trespass led to condemnation for all men, so one man's act of righteousness leads to

acquittal and life for all men. For as by one man's disobedience many were made sinners, so by one man's obedience many will be made righteous (Rm 5:18–19).

Christ, having fulfilled His mission, entrusted to His Church the task of sanctifying believers and, for this reason, most Christian denominations agree that sanctity or holiness is an essential and necessary characteristic of the Church Christ founded: *'But you are a chosen race, a royal priesthood, a holy nation, God's own people.'* (1P 2:9)

All things appropriated and dedicated to the worship of God are called holy and may not, by divine ordinance, be used for profane or worldly purposes. The profane use of anything consecrated for divine worship is called sacrilege.

> But no devoted thing that a man devotes to the Lord, of anything that he has, whether of man or beast, or of his inherited field, shall be sold or redeemed; every devoted thing is most holy to the Lord. No one devoted, who is to be utterly destroyed from among men, shall be ransomed; he shall be put to death. All the tithe of the land, whether of the seed of the land or of the fruit of the trees, is the Lord's; it is holy to the Lord (Lv 27:28–30).

Belshazzar committed sacrilege when he desecrated the Temple vessels by using them profanely at his great feast. He paid the supreme penalty for his effrontery:

> And you ..., Belshazzar, have not humbled your heart, ..., but you have lifted up yourself against the Lord of heaven; and the vessels of his house have been brought in before you, and you and your lords, your wives, and your concubines have drunk wine from them; and you have praised the gods of silver and gold, of bronze, iron, wood, and stone, which do not see or hear or know, but the God in whose hand is your breath, and whose are all your ways, you have not honoured. Then from his presence the hand was sent, and this writing was inscribed. And this is the writing that was inscribed: MENE, MENE, TEKEL, and PARSIN. This is the interpretation of

the matter: MENE, God has numbered the days of your kingdom and brought it to an end; TEKEL, you have been weighed in the balances and found wanting; PERES, your kingdom is divided and given to the Medes and Persians (Da 5:22–28).

Figure 16: *Daniel interprets Belshazzar's vision*

God is undoubtedly holy (Is 6:3) and the source of all holiness. *"For I am the Lord your God; consecrate yourselves therefore, and be holy, for I am holy"* (Lv 11:44). When the Word who is God '*became flesh and dwelt among us,*' He was '*full of grace and truth*' (Jn1:14) and, therefore, as head of the Church, could share His own holiness with the members of His body, the Church:

> For he who sanctifies and those who are sanctified have all one origin. That is why he is not ashamed to call them brethren, saying, 'I will proclaim thy name to my brethren, in the midst of the congregation I will praise thee.' And again, 'I will put my trust in him.' And again, 'Here am I, and the children God has given me' (Heb 2:11–13).

'*Since all have sinned and fall short of the glory of God*' (Rm 3:23), Christ founded His Church for the sake of sinners: '*I have not come to call the righteous, but sinners to repentance*' (Lk 5:32). Then, since God '*desires all men to be saved and to come to the knowledge of the truth*' (1Tm 2:4), Christ sanctified Himself so that His Church would be holy: '*for their sake I consecrate myself, that they also may be consecrated in truth*' (Jn 17:19). St Paul elaborated on this truth that all are '*called to be saints*' (1Co 1:2) when he wrote:

> Christ loved the church and gave himself up for her, that he might sanctify her, having cleansed her by the washing of water with the word, that he might present the church to himself in splendour, without spot or wrinkle or any such thing, that she might be holy and without blemish (Ep 5:25–27).

Human nature is so constituted that there is a direct correlation between behaviour and belief, that is, if people do not behave as they believe, they will believe as they behave. The teaching of sound doctrine is crucial for sustaining the moral behaviour, which is at the heart of holiness. St Paul, therefore, urged maturity in faith:

> … so that we may no longer be children, tossed to and fro and carried about with every wind of doctrine, by the cunning of men, by their craftiness in deceitful wiles. Rather, speaking the truth in love, we are to grow up in every way into him who is the head, into Christ, from whom the whole body, joined

and knit together by every joint with which it is supplied, when each part is working properly, makes bodily growth and upbuilds itself in love (Ep 4:14–16).

Holiness

Since '*they will be made holy who observe holy things in holiness*' (Ws 6:10) the seed of holiness is planted at Baptism when one is configured to Christ and incorporated as a member His Church: '*For as many of you as were baptised into Christ have put on Christ*' (Ga 3:27). Growth in holiness, however, comes from living the new life in Christ by struggling against the natural inclinations inherited from Adam: '*For while there is jealousy and strife among you, are you not of the flesh, and behaving like ordinary men?*' (1Co 3:3). Christ made the Church, which is His Body holy by the '*washing of water with the word*' (Ep 5:26), and, by His gifts of grace, calls her members to holiness:

> Blessed be the God and Father of our Lord Jesus Christ, who has blessed us in Christ with every spiritual blessing in the heavenly places, even as he chose us in him before the foundation of the world, that we should be holy and blameless before him (Ep 1:3–4).

A constant refrain sounded throughout Sacred Scripture is the call to be holy: '*as he who called you is holy, be holy yourselves in all your conduct; since it is written, 'You shall be holy, for I am holy*'' (1P 1:15–16). All members of the Church, therefore, are called to be saints '*that they may turn from darkness to light and from the power of Satan to God, that they may receive forgiveness of sins and a place among those who are sanctified by faith*' (Ac 26:18). In practice, this means that they must courageously face the daily struggle against sin: '*In your struggle against sin you have not yet resisted to the point of shedding your blood*' (Heb 12:4). Additionally, salvation is not achieved in a single step but, rather, the Christian has to *'work out his own salvation with fear and trembling'* (Ph 2:12). Since holiness is necessary for salvation, the Christian is urged to *'Strive ... for the holiness without which no one will see the Lord'* (Heb 12:14). Yet, since it is easy to fall into the trap of imagining that one is holy and already saved, St John warned about the dangers of self–deception when he wrote of the necessity of acknowledging one's sinfulness. By the confession of sin, one not only receives the forgiveness of one's sin but one is also able to avoid the danger of self-deception:

> If we say we have no sin, we deceive ourselves, and the truth is not in us. If we confess our sins, he is faithful and just, and will forgive our sins and cleanse us from all unrighteousness. If we say we have not sinned, we make him a liar, and his word is not in us (1Jn 1:8–10).

The Church embraces good and bad

Christ, in a number of parables, taught that the Church, His Body, would be composed of good and bad alike. In the parable of the wheat and chaff, Christ indicated that good as well as bad individuals would coexist in the Church until the end of time:

> The kingdom of heaven may be compared to a man who sowed good seed in his field; but while men were sleeping, his enemy came and sowed weeds among the wheat, and went away. So when the plants came up and bore grain, then the weeds appeared also. And the servants of the householder came and said to him, 'Sir, did you not sow good seed in your field? How then has it weeds?' He said to them, 'An enemy has done this.' The servants said to him, 'Then do you want us to go and gather them?' But he said, 'No; lest in gathering the weeds you root up the wheat along with them. Let both grow together until the harvest; and at harvest time I will tell the reapers, Gather the weeds first and bind

them in bundles to be burned, but gather the wheat into my barn' (Mt 13:24–30).

Although the Lord distributes gifts and talents according to ability, not all show the same zeal in using their gifts to the best of their ability as the parable of the faithful and unfaithful servants illustrates. A man entrusted his property to the care of three servants in proportion to their ability. Two of the servants invested the money given them and made a profit. The third servant, however, hid his talent. On the day of reckoning, the diligent servants were able to present the profit they had made and they received the correspondingly reward. The third servant, however

> … came forward, saying, 'Master, I knew you to be a hard man, reaping where you did not sow, and gathering where you did not winnow; so I was afraid, and I went and hid your talent in the ground. Here you have what is yours.' But his master answered him, 'You wicked and slothful servant! You knew that I reap where I have not sowed, and gather where I have not winnowed? Then you ought to have invested my money with the bankers, and at my coming I should have received what was my own with interest. So take the talent from him, and give it to him who has the ten talents. For to every one who has will more be given, and he will have abundance; but from him who has not, even what he has will be taken away. And cast the worthless servant into the outer darkness; there men will weep and gnash their teeth' (Mt 25:14–30).

In the parable of the wise and foolish virgins, Christ taught that faith as well as good works, symbolised by the lamp and oil respectively, are necessary for salvation.

> Then the kingdom of heaven shall be compared to ten maidens who took their lamps and went to meet the bridegroom. Five of them were foolish, and five were wise. For when the foolish took their lamps, they took no oil with them; but the wise took flasks of oil with their lamps. As the bridegroom was

delayed, they all slumbered and slept. But at midnight there was a cry, 'Behold, the bridegroom! Come out to meet him.' Then all those maidens rose and trimmed their lamps. And the foolish said to the wise, 'Give us some of your oil, for our lamps are going out.' But the wise replied, 'Perhaps there will not be enough for us and for you; go rather to the dealers and buy for yourselves.' And while they went to buy, the bridegroom came, and those who were ready went in with him to the marriage feast; and the door was shut. Afterward the other maidens came also, saying, 'Lord, Lord, open to us.' But he replied, 'Truly, I say to you, I do not know you.' Watch therefore, for you know neither the day nor the hour (Mt 25:1–13).

It is evident in the parable that all ten virgins were believers, that is, they all had faith. Christ, however, had commanded His disciples: '*Let your light so shine before men, that they may see your good works and give glory to your Father who is in heaven*' (Mt 5:16). Now, in much the same way that a lamp is fed by oil, so is faith fed and illumined by good works. This point St James passionately stressed when he wrote

What does it profit, my brethren, if a man says he has faith but has not works? Can his faith save him? If a brother or sister is ill–clad and in lack of daily food, and one of you says to them, 'Go in peace, be warmed and filled,' without giving them the things needed for the body, what does it profit? So faith by itself, if it has no works, is dead (Jm 2:14–17).

It can be deduced, therefore, that the five foolish virgins were refused entry into eternal life because either they did not have sufficient good works to their credit, or they had performed good works for the wrong reasons as Christ had warned against. '*Beware of practicing your piety before men in order to be seen by them; for then you will have no reward from your Father who is in heaven*' (Mt 6:1). The point, however, that St James made is that '*a man is justified by works and not by faith alone'* (Jm 2:24) and *'as the body apart from the spirit is dead, so faith apart from works is dead'* (Jm 2:26).

The Church in this world, like the dragnet catching good and bad fish, embraces all who enter her fold:

> Again, the kingdom of heaven is like a net which was thrown into the sea and gathered fish of every kind; when it was full, men drew it ashore and sat down and sorted the good into vessels but threw away the bad. So it will be at the close of the age. The angels will come out and separate the evil from the righteous, and throw them into the furnace of fire; there men will weep and gnash their teeth (Mt 13:47–50).

Christ established His Church to continue His own mission of calling sinners to repentance. The Church He founded, consequently, embraces sinners within her fold, where they receive the ministrations of the Father. Christ had taught that the Father's care for the vineyard is unremitting and that each tree is dealt with individually as the following parable illustrates:

> A man had a fig tree planted in his vineyard; and he came seeking fruit on it and found none. And he said to the vinedresser, 'Lo, these three years I have come seeking fruit on this fig tree, and I find none. Cut it down; why should it use up the ground?' And he answered him, 'Let it alone, sir, this year also, till I dig about it and put on manure. And if it bears fruit next year, well and good; but if not, you can cut it down' (Lk 13:6–9).

Although the Apostles reproved Christians whose external conduct was at variance with their professed faith, they never suggest that these Christians were not members of the Church. Christ, in fact, specifically chose Judas as an Apostle although, He was fully aware of Judas' true character *'For Jesus knew from the first who those were that did not believe, and who it was that would betray him'* (Jn 6:64). He even openly stated that, among the Apostles whom He chose, there were good and bad men: *''Did I not choose you, the twelve, and one of you is a devil?' He spoke of Judas the son of Simon Iscariot, for he, one of the twelve, was to betray him'* (Jn 6:70–71). Later on, He would give His disciples an example to follow by calling Judas 'friend' at the very moment that Judas was executing his act of treachery:

> Judas came, one of the twelve, and with him a great crowd with swords and clubs, from the chief priests and the elders of the people. Now the betrayer had given them a sign, saying, 'The one I shall kiss is the man; seize him.' And he came up to Jesus at once and said, 'Hail, Master!' And he kissed him. Jesus said to him, 'Friend, why are you here?' (Mt 26:47–50)

Figure 17: *Judas betrays Christ*

Christ came to call sinners to repentance and this included Judas. Therefore, by extending the hand of friendship, Christ left the door open for Judas to return, if he wished.

Judas chose otherwise, and even though he was '*a thief, and as he had the money box he used to take what was put into it*' (Jn 12:6), his ministry, however, remained valid. St Peter threw no aspersions on its validity but rather, he openly declared, '*For he was numbered among us, and was allotted his share in this ministry*' (Ac 1:17).

There is no doubt that serious personal sin makes one a dead member of the Church though there always remains the hope of conversion:

> And you, who once were estranged and hostile in mind, doing evil deeds, he has now reconciled in his body of flesh by his death, in order to present you holy and blameless and irreproachable before him, provided that you continue in the faith, stable and steadfast, not shifting from the hope of the gospel which you heard (Col 1:21–23).

Additionally, personal sin does not invalidate the exercise of authority in the Church since ultimately all authority comes from God. St Peter's experience is instructive: despite his three-fold denial of his association with the Lord, Christ's love for him remained intact. A single look of compassion from Christ was sufficient to draw bitter tears from a contrite Peter.

> Peter followed at a distance; and when they had kindled a fire in the middle of the courtyard and sat down together, Peter sat among them. Then a maid, seeing him as he sat in the light and gazing at him, said, 'This man also was with him.' But he denied it, saying, 'Woman, I do not know him.' And a little later some one else saw him and said, 'You also are one of them.' But Peter said, 'Man, I am not.' And after an interval of about an hour still another insisted, saying, 'Certainly this man also was with him; for he is a Galilean.' But Peter said, 'Man, I do not know what you are saying.' And immediately, while he was still speaking, the cock crowed. And the Lord turned and looked at Peter. And Peter remembered the word of the Lord, how he had said

to him, 'Before the cock crows today, you will deny me three times.' And he went out and wept bitterly (Lk 22:54–62).

Figure 18: *St Peter denies Christ*

Simon Peter, however, was not the only disciple to fail Christ on the night of His betrayal. In fact, when Christ was arrested, the Apostles, as a group, *'all forsook him, and fled'* (Mk 14:50). Only John the beloved disciple was at Calvary with the women. *'But standing by the cross of Jesus were his mother, and his mother's sister, Mary the wife of Clopas, and Mary Magdalene. … Jesus saw his mother, and the disciple whom he loved standing near'* (Jn 19:25–26). After His Resurrection on the third day, Christ appeared to His Apostles in the Upper Room and, far from upbraiding them for their cowardice and infidelity, confirmed their apostolate:

> On the evening of that day, the first day of the week, the doors being shut where the disciples were, for fear of the Jews, Jesus came and stood among them and said to them, 'Peace be with you.' When he had said this, he showed them his hands and his side. Then the disciples were glad when they saw the

Lord. Jesus said to them again, 'Peace be with you. As the Father has sent me, even so I send you.' And when he had said this, he breathed on them, and said to them, 'Receive the Holy Spirit. If you forgive the sins of any, they are forgiven; if you retain the sins of any, they are retained' (Jn 20:19–23).

'*Since all have sinned and fall short of the glory of God*' (Rm 3:23), everyone stands in need of forgiveness as well as to be reconciled to God. By His death, Christ fulfilled His mission and made reparation for every sin. Now, having risen from the dead, Christ bestowed the benediction '*peace be with you*' on His Apostles and, in this way, restored them from being dead members to living members of the Church He founded. They were to go out and preach this forgiveness and reconciliation to the whole world until the end of time.

Points to Remember

a. *Since all human beings are sinners, they all stand in need of salvation.*

b. *Christ founded a Church that would embrace sinners and transform them into saints.*

c. *The Church is holy because Christ, her head, is holy and because her teachings, sacraments and morality lead to holiness.*

d. *Through Baptism, one becomes a member of the Church. Personal sin cannot destroy this membership but it does make one a dead member of the Church.*

e. *All members of Christ's Church are called to be saints and must work out their salvation with 'fear and trembling'.*

9

The Church Christ founded is Catholic

Preamble

Christ established one Church for the salvation of the entire human race. Embracing all nations, peoples, races, tongues and social classes, she teaches them the same universal truths delivered by Christ to the Apostles and offers one single sacrifice to God for the forgiveness of sin. Catholicity requires that the Church Christ founded enjoys a three-fold universality, namely, that, by encompassing all nations she is everywhere geographically, that her doctrines are the same everywhere and that they have not changed substantially with time.

Exposition

The term 'catholic' means universal in the sense of 'in respect of the whole'. Although the word 'catholic' is not found in the Bible, nonetheless, its meaning is contained in Christ's words when He commissioned His apostles to '*Go therefore and make disciples of all nations, ... teaching them to observe all that I have commanded you; and lo, I am with you always, to the close of the age*' (Mt 28:19–20). Having founded His Church for the salvation of the human race, Christ determined, also, that it might preserve His revelation unchanged and dispense His grace to people of all nations.

Hence, it is necessary that His Church should be found in every land, proclaiming His message to all human beings and communicating to them the means of grace. The Church, then, is Catholic in a double sense: first, as Christ's Mystical Body and secondly, as having a universal mission.

As Christ's body, the Church receives from Him, who is *'the head over all things ... the fullness of him who fills all in all'* (Ep 1:22–23), the fullness of the means of salvation. This fullness consists in the correct and complete confession of faith, a full sacramental life and an ordained ministry *'of Christ Jesus ... in the priestly service of the gospel of God'* (Rm 15:16). In this fundamental sense, the Church became Catholic on the day of Pentecost and will remain so until Christ returns:

> I looked, and behold, a great multitude which no man could number, from every nation, from all tribes and peoples and tongues, standing before the throne and before the Lamb, clothed in white robes, with palm branches in their hands (Rev 7:9).

Having received her mission from Christ, the Church was sent out with an undertaking to the whole human race. The mission was initiated on the day of Pentecost, when the Apostles, filled with the Holy Spirit, preached to the devout men of every nation living in Jerusalem in their own language. Thus, the glorious work of redemption that God had begun among them was revealed to

> Parthians and Medes and Elamites and residents of Mesopotamia, Judea and Cappadocia, Pontus and Asia, Phrygia and Pamphylia, Egypt and the parts of Libya belonging to Cyrene, and visitors from Rome, both Jews and proselytes, Cretans and Arabians, we hear them telling in our own tongues the mighty works of God (Ac 2:9–11).

The preaching of the Apostles led to the conversion and baptism of some three thousand people from among the various nations represented in Jerusalem on that day. Therefore, from her beginning, the Church embraced all nations, all peoples, all languages and all social classes.

Later on, because of the missionary work of Barnabas and Paul, the Church expanded rapidly among the Gentiles so that the Apostles found it necessary to meet in Council with Barnabas and Paul to determine whether the Gentiles were required to observe the Mosaic Law. At this Council, held in Jerusalem, it was then recognised that the Gentiles were not to become Jews, but rather, they were called by God, together with the Jews to become, *'one new man in place of the two'* (Ep 2:15). That is, God had reconciled them in one body, the one Church, which subsists in all ages, teaches all nations, and is the one ark of salvation for all, as prophesied by Amos 9:11 and quoted by St James:

> And all the assembly kept silence; and they listened to Barnabas and Paul as they related what signs and wonders God had done through them among the Gentiles. After they finished speaking, James replied, 'Brethren, listen to me. Simeon has related how God first visited the Gentiles, to take out of them a people for his name. And with this the words of the prophets agree, as it is written, 'After this I will return, and I will rebuild the dwelling of David, which has fallen; I will rebuild its ruins, and I will set it up, that the rest of men may seek the Lord, and all the Gentiles who are called by my name, says the Lord, who has made these things known from of old' (Ac 15:12–18).

The principal effect of Adam's sin was to bring about the universal condemnation of the human race, which could only be remedied by Christ's act of reparation: *'Then as one man's trespass led to condemnation for all men, so one man's act of righteousness leads to acquittal and life for all men'* (Rm 5:18). To undo Adam's sin, Christ, in the fullness of time, *'came and preached peace to you who were far off and peace to those who were near'* (Ep 2:17) and established His Church, *'built on the foundation of the apostles and prophets'* (Ep 2:20), whereby the effects of His act of reparation might be applied to all those professing the true faith, from Adam to the present day, and even to those yet to be born.

Prophets foresaw Church's catholicity

The Church's catholicity or universality was foreseen by various Old Testament prophets. Thus, for instance, David prophesied in Psalm 2 the coming of Christ and His kingdom, the Church. The catholicity of the kingdom, which embraces all nations is seen in this Messianic psalm, where Christ, *'the Lord's anointed'*, through the victory of His cross, obtained, by right of conquest, power over all the nations: *'Ask of me, and I will make the nations your heritage and the ends of the earth your possession'* (Ps 2:8). In another messianic psalm, the nations come to Him in family groups to worship in the unity of the one faith on Mount Zion: *'All the ends of the earth shall remember and turn to the Lord; and all the families of the nations shall worship before him'* (Ps 22:27). This theme is echoed in Psalm 87, which foresaw the Church as the true Zion, the kingdom that God established as the mother of all the redeemed:

> Among those who know me I mention Rahab and Babylon; behold, Philistia and Tyre, with Ethiopia. This one was born there, they say. And of Zion it shall be said, 'This one and that one were born in her'; for the Most High himself will establish her (Ps 87:4–5).

In a dream, the prophet Daniel saw the Messiah being awarded a universal kingdom or empire that was catholic and indestructible: *'And to him was given dominion and glory and kingdom, that all peoples, nations, and languages should serve him; his dominion is an everlasting dominion, which shall not pass away, and his kingdom one that shall not be destroyed'* (Da 7:14).

In his first letter, St Peter clearly taught not only that Noah's ark, through which the human race was preserved during the Flood, prefigured the Church and the sacrament of Baptism, but also that Christ went to the underworld to preach the Gospel to the dead. In this way, salvation is made available to the whole human race from creation until Christ's second coming:

> For Christ also died for sins once for all, the righteous for the unrighteous, that he might bring us to God, being put to death in the flesh but made alive in the spirit; in which he went and preached to the spirits in prison, who formerly did not obey, when God's patience waited in the days of Noah, during the building of the ark, in which a few, that is, eight persons, were saved through water. Baptism, which corresponds to this, now saves you, not as a removal of dirt from the body but as an appeal to God for a clear conscience, through the resurrection of Jesus Christ (1P 3:18–21).

Figure 19: *The dove returns to Noah's ark with the olive branch*

Jerusalem, the place of sacrifice

Long before the Israelites had taken possession of the Promised Land, God had determined that the earthly Jerusalem should be the only lawful place for offering Him sacrifice:

> then to the place which the Lord your God will choose, to make his name dwell there, thither you shall bring all that I command you: your burnt offerings and your sacrifices, your tithes and the offering that you present, and all your votive offerings which you vow to the Lord. ... Take heed that you do not offer your burnt offerings at every place that you see; but at the place which the Lord will choose in one of your tribes, there you shall offer your burnt offerings, and there you shall do all that I am commanding you.. but you shall eat them before the Lord your God in the place which the Lord your God will choose (Dt 12:11–14).

Figure 20: *Building the Temple in Jerusalem*

The Psalmist exalted that God did indeed choose Jerusalem as this place: *'For the Lord has chosen Zion; he has desired it for his habitation: "This is my resting place for ever; here I will dwell, for I have desired it"'* (Ps 132:13–14). However, because of Solomon's infidelity, God divided the kingdom but, as He told Jeroboam, *'to his son I will give one tribe, that David my servant may always have a lamp before me in Jerusalem, the city where I have chosen to put my name'* (1K 11:36). This knowledge makes it clear why Jeroboam's establishment of places of sacrifice outside of Jerusalem was an abomination to the Lord. Further, since the earthly Jerusalem was a type and foreshadowing of the Church, it is natural that the Church should now be the only true place of worship. Christ intimated this when He told the woman of Samaria *'the hour is coming, and now is, when the true worshippers will worship the Father in spirit and truth, for such the Father seeks to worship him'* (Jn 4:23). The prefiguration is also evident from the offering of Melchizedek, the priest king of Salem (later to become Jerusalem), a sacrificial offering of bread and wine, and his receiving tithes from the patriarch Abram:

> Melchizedek king of Salem brought out bread and wine; he was priest of God Most High. And he blessed him and said, 'Blessed be Abram by God Most High, maker of heaven and earth; and blessed be God Most High, who has delivered your enemies into your hand!' And Abram gave him a tenth of everything (Gn 14:18–20).

In receiving the blessing and giving tithes, Abram made a threefold acknowledgement of Melchizedek's superiority: first as a priest since *'It is beyond dispute that the inferior is blessed by the superior'* (Heb 7:7), second, because of the eminence of the place of sacrifice, *'Jerusalem, … the city of the great King'* (Mt 5:35), and third, from the greatness of the bread and wine sacrifice he offered. *'For it is impossible that the blood of bulls and goats should take away sins'* (Heb 10:4).

Now, the true sacrifice acceptable to God is Christ who *'entered once for all into the Holy Place, taking not the blood of* goats and calves but his own blood, thus securing an eternal redemption' (Heb 9:12). This selfsame sacrifice is offered, under the appearances of bread and wine, in the Church, which is the heavenly Jerusalem visible on earth: *'But you have come to Mount Zion and to the city of the living God, the heavenly Jerusalem, and to innumerable angels in festal gathering'* (Heb 12:22). In the Church, the baptised *'have confidence to enter the sanctuary by the blood of Jesus, by the new and living way which he opened … through the curtain, that is, through his flesh'* (Heb 10:19–20). There, they are called and able to offer the one, and only, sacrifice acceptable to God and so fulfil the prophecy of Malachi:

> For from the rising of the sun to its setting my name is great among the nations, and in every place incense is offered to my name, and a pure offering; for my name is great among the nations, says the Lord of hosts (Ml 1:11).

Called *'the inheritance of God'* (Ps 2:8) and *'the people of God'* (Os.2:1), the Church Christ founded is to prepare a people fit for the Lord (Lk 1:17). Her children have no permanent dwelling place in this world but, rather, they look *'forward to the city which has foundations, whose builder and maker is God'* (Heb 11:10) and, by imitating Christ, they *'go forth to him outside the camp and bear the abuse he endured. For here we have no lasting city, but we seek the city which is to come'* (Heb 13:13–14).

The Church, then, since she embraces all nations, all peoples, all races, all tongues, all classes, is catholic or universal in time because Christ promised that she would never fail: *'I will build my church, and the gates of hell shall not prevail against it'* (Mt 16:18). She is universal in place since, in addition to making *'disciples of all nations, baptising them in the name of the Father and of the Son and of the Holy Spirit,'* (Mt 28:19) she also holds them within her embrace, so that *'there is neither Jew nor Greek, there is neither slave nor free, there is neither male nor female; for you are all one in Christ Jesus'* (Ga 3:28). She is universal in doctrine because she teaches the entire and undiluted doctrine of Christ: *'teaching them to observe all that I have commanded you; and lo, I am with you always, to the close of the age'* (Mt 28:20).

Points to Remember

a. *Christ founded one Church to teach the whole human race the same universal truths and to offer one single sacrifice to the one God.*

b. *This Church embraces all nations, peoples, tongues and classes of people.*

c. *The Church offers one single acceptable sacrifice to God.*

d. *The Church Christ founded is universal in time and space.*

10

The Church Christ founded is Apostolic

Preamble

Apostolicity is logically the first of the four characteristics of the Church Christ founded since the apostolic Church must have been one, holy and catholic. Christ chose twelve Apostles at the beginning of His ministry and, for three years, He taught and trained them. They were eyewitnesses to all the things He said and did. After His resurrection from the dead, He appeared to them and commissioned them to teach the message of the redemption to all nations. Once they had received the gift of the Holy Spirit at Pentecost, the Apostles boldly preached the message of Christ's death and resurrection to the Jewish people. They declared themselves witnesses who had eaten and drunk with Him after His resurrection. With Simon Peter as their recognised and undisputed leader, they formed the nucleus of the Church and, as leaders, taught and exercised authority and they were, in turn, obeyed.

Apostleship is not merely a preaching ministry but rather, an office of authority that Christ established as an constitutive part of His Church. Consequently, the basis of apostolic authority was not each Apostle's personal influence but his apostleship. If it were otherwise, Peter, the humble, uneducated Galilean fisherman, would not have been able to retain his pre-eminent position against Paul, the learned and formidable Pharisee and Roman citizen. The Apostles, then, were fully aware that the authority and office given to them were for the good of the Church Christ founded and they made provision for the future by laying hands on other men who were to share in their apostolate, to exercise the apostolic authority and office and to succeed them. The successors of the Apostles are the bishops of the Church Christ founded.

Exposition

At the onset of His public ministry, Christ, after spending a night in prayer, deliberately chose '*those whom he desired; and they came to him. And he appointed twelve, to be with him, and to be sent out to preach and have authority to cast out demons*' (Mk 3:13–19). These twelve men formed the apostolic College on which the Church was to be founded. They were also to continue Christ's work of redemption by going out into the world to bear fruit for eternal life: '*You did not choose me, but I chose you and appointed you that you should go and bear fruit and that your fruit should abide*' (Jn 15:1). The fruit they were to bear was to complete what the prophets before them had begun, which was the ingathering of souls for the kingdom.

> Jesus said to them, 'My food is to do the will of him who sent me, and to accomplish his work. Do you not say, 'There are yet four months, then comes the harvest?' I tell you, lift up your eyes, and see how the fields are already white for harvest. He who reaps receives wages, and gathers fruit for eternal life, so that sower and reaper may rejoice together. For here the saying holds true, 'One sows and another reaps.' I sent you to reap that for which you did not labour; others have laboured, and you have entered into their labour' (Jn 4:34–38).

The Apostles were the official witnesses primarily to the life, death and Resurrection of Christ, who had chosen them to be His representatives in the world into which He would send them. Essentially, a witness is a person who sees an incident as it takes place and is able to swear to the fact of it happening. *'Truly, truly, I say to you, we speak of what we know, and bear witness to what we have seen'* (Jn 3:11).

On the day of His Resurrection, Christ appeared to the Apostles in the Upper Room and opened their minds to understand that He had fulfilled the Scriptures in His own person and mission and that they had been eyewitnesses of all that He had done. *'He said to them, "Thus it is written, that the Christ should suffer and on the third day rise from the dead ... You are witnesses of these things"'* (Lk 24:46–48). Over the next forty days, He proved the reality of His Resurrection by appearing to them, eating with them and giving them further instruction on the purpose of His mission and the nature of the Church He founded. *'To them he presented himself alive after his passion by many proofs, appearing to them during forty days, and speaking of the kingdom of God'* (Ac 1:3). Before His ascension into heaven, He promised them the assistance of the Holy Spirit and reconfirmed their commission as witnesses to the whole world: *'But you shall receive power when the Holy Spirit has come upon you; and you shall be my witnesses in Jerusalem and in all Judea and Samaria and to the end of the earth'* (Ac 1:8).

The Apostles were fully aware that their primary task was to witness to Christ's death and Resurrection. They also knew that God had already chosen Judas' replacement. They therefore decided, as a criterion, that the person replacing Judas should have been with Jesus from His baptism until His ascension and, above all, be a witness to His Resurrection.

> So one of the men who have accompanied us during all the time that the Lord Jesus went in and out among us, beginning from the baptism of John until the day when he was taken up from us—one of these

> men must become with us a witness to his resurrection. And they put forward two, Joseph called Barsabbas, who was surnamed Justus, and Matthias. And they prayed and said, 'Lord, who knowest the hearts of all men, show which one of these two thou hast chosen to take the place in this ministry and apostleship from which Judas turned aside, to go to his own place.' And they cast lots for them, and the lot fell on Matthias; and he was enrolled with the eleven apostles (Ac 1: 21–26).

In their confrontation with the Jewish authorities, the Apostles were clear about their status and they openly declared the reality of Christ's Resurrection: '*This Jesus God raised up, and of that we all are witnesses*' (Ac 2:32).

As leaders, the Apostles were the public and official witnesses in the Church. They represented Christ and spoke in His name and, ultimately, in God's name. '*He who hears you hears me, and he who rejects you rejects me, and he who rejects me rejects him who sent me*' (Lk 10:16). On the night of His betrayal, Christ told them '*you also are witnesses, because you have been with me from the beginning*' (Jn 15:27), and the Apostles boldly affirmed their status before the Jewish Sanhedrin: '*And we are witnesses to these things, and so is the Holy Spirit whom God has given to those who obey him*' (Ac 5:32). In his encounter with Cornelius in Joppa, Simon Peter told Cornelius the things Jesus had done and concluded by saying he was speaking from his own personal experience, that is, as a witness:

> we are witnesses to all that he did both in the country of the Jews and in Jerusalem. They put him to death by hanging him on a tree; but God raised him on the third day and made him manifest; not to all the people but to us who were chosen by God as witnesses, who ate and drank with him after he rose from the dead (Ac 10:39–41).

In the synagogue at Antioch in Pisidia, St Paul summarised basic Jewish history to show that the Old Testament prophecies were fulfilled in Christ Jesus. He concluded by saying that God raised Christ from the dead and that the Apostles were witnesses to this: *'for many days he appeared to those who came up with him from Galilee to Jerusalem, who are now his witnesses to the people'* (Ac 13:31).

Christ commissioned His Apostles to preach the Gospel to all nations. That is, they were to proclaim to all nations the death and Resurrection of Christ, which reveals the essential goodness and love of

> the Father, who has qualified us to share in the inheritance of the saints in light. He has delivered us from the dominion of darkness and transferred us to the kingdom of his beloved Son, in whom we have redemption, the forgiveness of sins (Col 1:12–14).

St Paul the Apostle

Christ, likewise, commissioned St Paul on the day He appeared to him on the road to Damascus. St Paul was to be a servant and a witness: *'The Lord said ... "I have appeared to you for this purpose, to appoint you to serve and bear witness to the things in which you have seen me and to those in which I will appear to you"'* (Ac 26:15–18). In defending the legitimacy of his apostleship, St Paul told the Galatians that the Gospel he preached came straight from Christ. *'For I would have you know, brethren, that the gospel which was preached by me is not man's gospel. For I did not receive it from man, nor was I taught it, but it came through a revelation of Jesus Christ'* (Ga 1:11–12). In this way, he ranks himself with the Twelve, who accepted the validity and legitimacy of his apostleship.

He further declared that

> those, I say, who were of repute added nothing to me; but on the contrary, when they saw that I had been entrusted with the gospel to the uncircumcised, just as Peter had been entrusted with the gospel to the circumcised (for he who worked through Peter for the mission to the circumcised worked through me also for the Gentiles), and when they perceived

> the grace that was given to me, James and Cephas
> and John, who were reputed to be pillars, gave to
> me and Barnabas the right hand of fellowship, that
> we should go to the Gentiles and they to the circum-
> cised (Ga 2:6–9).

St Paul saw himself, first and foremost, as a servant of Christ
entrusted with mysteries, which he faithfully dispensed to
those to whom he had been sent. *'This is how one should
regard us, as servants of Christ and stewards of the mysteries of
God. Moreover it is required of stewards that they be found
trustworthy'* (1Co 4:1). Although he had to face continual
opposition from *'false brethren secretly brought in'* (Ga 2:4) he
did not lose heart. Instead, he courageously and zealously
strove to fulfil his commission by being a faithful dispenser
of the mysteries of God.

> Therefore, having this ministry by the mercy of God,
> we do not lose heart. We have renounced
> disgraceful, underhanded ways; we refuse to prac-
> tice cunning or to tamper with God's word, but by
> the open statement of the truth we would commend
> ourselves to every man's conscience in the sight of
> God. And even if our gospel is veiled, it is veiled
> only to those who are perishing. … For what we
> preach is not ourselves, but Jesus Christ as Lord,
> with ourselves as your servants for Jesus' sake (2Co
> 4:1–5).

He regarded and carried out his commission as an obligation and a responsibility for which he expected no earthly
reward. *'For necessity is laid upon me. Woe to me if I do not
preach the gospel! For if I do this of my own will, I have a reward;
but if not of my own will, I am entrusted with a commission'* (1Co
9:16–17).

St Paul claimed that his apostleship gave him the right
to speak in the name of Christ, that is, as an ambassador. It
was in that capacity that he asked the Ephesians to make
supplication *'also for me, that utterance may be given me in
opening my mouth boldly to proclaim the mystery of the gospel,*

for which I am an ambassador in chains; that I may declare it boldly, as I ought to speak' (Ep 6:20).

As an apostle of Christ, St Paul had the right to command but, as a servant of Christ, he encouraged people to do the right thing out of the goodness of their heart. Hence, he wrote to Philemon *'though I am bold enough in Christ to command you to do what is required, yet for love's sake I prefer to appeal to you—I, Paul, an ambassador and now a prisoner also for Christ Jesus— I appeal to you'* (Phm 8–10).

Although Christ promised to be with His Church until the end of time, He did not promise the Apostles that they would remain alive until His return. In fact, He told them that they would have to endure persecution, and even death, on His account.

> Beware of men; for they will deliver you up to councils, and flog you in their synagogues, and you will be dragged before governors and kings for my sake, to bear testimony before them and the Gentiles. When they deliver you up, do not be anxious how you are to speak or what you are to say; for what you are to say will be given to you in that hour; for it is not you who speak, but the Spirit of your Father speaking through you. Brother will deliver up brother to death, and the father his child, and children will rise against parents and have them put to death; and you will be hated by all for my name's sake (Mt 10:17–22).

The fulfilment of this prophecy began when Herod *'killed James the brother of John with the sword'* (Acts 12:2). Since the Apostles themselves were subject to death, it is necessary that their office and spirit continue in the Church for the fulfilment of Christ's promise that His Church would last until the end of time. Men who had not been with Christ during His earthly life, such as Barnabas and Saul, were, therefore, chosen for the apostolic office: *'While they were worshiping the Lord and fasting, the Holy Spirit said, "Set apart for me Barnabas and Saul for the work to which I have called them"'* (Ac 13:2). They, in turn, would choose other men, such as Timothy and Titus to share in the apostolic ministry: *'what you have heard from me before many witnesses entrust to faithful men who will be able to teach others also'* (2Tm 2:2).

The apostolic office was transmitted by the laying-on of hands: *'Do not neglect the gift you have, which was given you by prophetic utterance when the council of elders laid their hands upon you.'* (1Tm 4:14) The successors of the Apostles were called bishops and they carried out the same mission and exercised the same authority as the Apostles themselves.

> This is why I left you in Crete, that you might amend what was defective, and appoint elders in every town as I directed you, if any man is blameless, the husband of one wife, and his children are believers and not open to the charge of being profligate or insubordinate. For a bishop, as God's steward, must be blameless; he must not be arrogant or quick–tempered or a drunkard or violent or greedy for gain, but hospitable, a lover of goodness, master of himself, upright, holy, and self–controlled; he must hold firm to the sure word as taught, so that he may be able to give instruction in sound doctrine and also to confute those who contradict it (Tt 1:5–9).

The Apostles had the authority and power to ordain other suitable men to the ministry. The Apostles, in fact, did ordain such men with the understanding that those so chosen were to receive, to hold on to, and to hand on the apostolic teaching intact as they, the Apostles themselves, had received it. Since this ministerial ordination was an apostolic act, the men so ordained would, likewise, be able to ordain other men to succeed them and to hand on that same authority and power they had received from the Apostles. This is what is meant by the apostolic succession.

Christ gave the Apostles authority to decide disputes between Church members and to take action against the rebellious. *'If he refuses to listen to them, tell it to the church; and if he refuses to listen even to the church, let him be to you as a Gentile and a tax collector'* (Mt 18:17). Thus, the apostolic College would be the highest court of appeal. Further, since the Apostles were *'ambassadors for Christ'* (2Co 5:20), obedience to them was obedience to Him: *'Truly, truly, I say to you, he who receives anyone whom I send receives me; and he who receives me receives him who sent me'* (Jn 13:20). The Apostles exercised then supreme authority in the Church and, in all matters relating to the faith and spiritual life, were obeyed. *'Therefore, my beloved, as you have always obeyed, so now, not only as in my presence but much more in my absence'* (Ph 2:12).

True apostleship

An apostle is one who is sent forth. The Apostles were sent as teachers of doctrine, priests of divine worship and ministers of governance by Jesus Christ who, Himself being sent by the Father, is called the *'the apostle and high priest of our confession'* (Heb 3:1). It is abundantly clear from Christ's teaching and example that a true apostle does not speak or act in his own name but rather in the name of the one who sent him:

> Jesus answered them, 'My teaching is not mine, but his who sent me; if any man's will is to do his will, he shall know whether the teaching is from God or whether I am speaking on my own authority. He who speaks on his own authority seeks his own glory; but he who seeks the glory of him who sent him is true, and in him there is no falsehood' (Jn 7:16–18).

Christ affirmed on many occasions that He did not act on His own authority but rather on the authority of the Father who sent Him (Jn 5:27; 6:38; 8:28; 12:49). In particular, He stated, *'I can do nothing on my own authority; as I hear, I judge; and my judgment is just, because I seek not my own will but the will of him who sent me'* (Jn 5:30). Since, however, His testimony was not accepted, He substantiated His claim by bringing forward many witnesses. These witnesses included first, John the Baptist *'You sent to John, and he has borne witness to the truth'* (Jn 5:33). Second, the works He Himself had performed *'But the testimony which I have is greater than that of John; for the works which the Father has granted me to accomplish, these very works which I am doing, bear me witness that the Father has sent me'* (Jn 5:36); and *'The works that I do in my Father's name, they bear witness to me'* (Jn 10:25; see Jn 10:38; 14:11). Third, the Father who sent Him: *'And the Father who sent me has himself borne witness to me'* (Jn 5:37; see also Jn 8:18). Fourth, the Scriptures: *'You search the scriptures, because you think that in them you have eternal life; and it is they that bear witness to me'* (Jn 5:39). Fifth, Moses: *'If you believed Moses, you would believe me, for he wrote of me. But if you do not believe his writings, how will you believe my words?'* (Jn 5:46–47). His final testimony that all authority emanates from the divine will was made before Pontius Pilate to whom He said, *'You would have no power over me unless it had been given you from above'* (Jn 19:11). Both St Peter (1P 2:13) and St Paul (Rm 13) would later expound and draw out the practical consequences flowing from this doctrine about the source of authority. To sum up, there is only one Source for all authority and, from this derives the authority and activity of Christ and His Apostles, and that of the Holy Spirit:

> When the Spirit of truth comes, he will guide you into all the truth; for he will not speak on his own authority, but whatever he hears he will speak, and he will declare to you the things that are to come (Jn 16:13).

Christ's authority, which extends over all creation, originates directly from the fact that

> He is the image of the invisible God, the first–born of all creation; for in him all things were created, in heaven and on earth, visible and invisible, whether thrones or dominions or principalities or authorities– –all things were created through him and for him. He is before all things, and in him all things hold together (Col 1:15–17).

He openly and explicitly declared this to His Apostles *'All authority in heaven and on earth has been given to me'* (Mt 28:18) and with this same authority, He commissioned them *'As thou didst send me into the world, so I have sent them into the world'* (Jn 17:18). Aware, however, that after His ascension a counterfeit authority would make its appearance, Christ warned the Jews *'I have come in my Father's name, and you do not receive me; if another comes in his own name, him you will receive'* (Jn 5:43). He likewise warned His disciples to be vigilant since even His name would be used to deceive them: *'For many will come in my name, saying, 'I am the Christ,' and they will lead many astray'* (Mt 24:5). The point was driven home at Ephesus by the demons who overcame some Jewish exorcists acting without apostolic mandate.

> Then some of the itinerant Jewish exorcists under-took to pronounce the name of the Lord Jesus over those who had evil spirits, saying, 'I adjure you by the Jesus whom Paul preaches.' Seven sons of a Jewish high priest named Sceva were doing this. But the evil spirit answered them, 'Jesus I know, and Paul I know; but who are you?' And the man in whom the evil spirit was leaped on them, mastered all of them, and overpowered them, so that they fled out of that house naked and wounded (Ac 19:13–16).

In the things pertaining to God's service *'one does not take the honour upon himself, but he is called by God, just as Aaron was'* (Heb 5:4). Now since the apostolic office is an extension of Christ's redemptive mission, the Apostles had to be chosen personally by Christ Himself. St Paul frequently defended his call to the apostolic dignity, declaring, *'For this gospel I was appointed a preacher and apostle and teacher, and therefore I suffer as I do'* (2Tm 1:11–12). He even identifies himself with Christ when castigating the Corinthians *'since you desire proof that Christ is speaking in me.'* (2Co 13:3) Painfully aware that some were falsely claiming apostolic rank for themselves, he did not hesitate to denounce them in order to protect the faithful:

> And what I do I will continue to do, in order to undermine the claim of those who would like to claim that in their boasted mission they work on the

same terms as we do. For such men are false apostles, deceitful workmen, disguising themselves as apostles of Christ. And no wonder, for even Satan disguises himself as an angel of light. So it is not strange if his servants also disguise themselves as servants of righteousness. Their end will correspond to their deeds (2Co 11:12–15).

Then, since it is better to light a candle than to curse the darkness, St Paul identified the characteristics of true apostleship both to expose the imposters and to arm the faithful against their deceptions.

The task of '*building up the body of Christ*' (Ep 4:11–12) requires so many different offices that '*God has appointed in the church first apostles, second prophets, third teachers, then workers of miracles, then healers, helpers, administrators, speakers in various kinds of tongues.*' (1Co 12:28) Now because of the importance of the apostolic office for the mission of the Church, it was necessary that it be secured from infiltration by imposters. To ensure this and to nullify the claims, incursions and deprecations of false apostles, St Paul highlighted the five characteristics possessed by a true Apostle.

Credentials of a true Apostle

First, since Christ commissioned Jews only, an Apostle must be a Jew. St Paul showed that like the Twelve, he possessed this credential: '*Are they Hebrews? So am I. Are they Israelites? So am I. Are they descendants of Abraham? So am I*' (2Co 11:22).

Second, the New Testament records that after His Resurrection Christ appeared to the women, to the Apostles individually and collectively, as well as to five hundred of the disciples (1Co 15:6). St Paul argued from this that a personal visual encounter with the risen Lord is a necessary criterion for true apostleship.

Am I not an apostle? Have I not seen Jesus our Lord? Are not you my workmanship in the Lord? If to others

> I am not an apostle, at least I am to you; for you are
> the seal of my apostleship in the Lord (1Co 9:1–2).

Third, an Apostle must be a servant of Christ. Throughout his epistles, St Paul claimed to be Christ's servant and held out his many sufferings for the sake of the Gospel as proof that he was a better servant than the false apostles claimed themselves to be *'Are they servants of Christ? I am a better one … with far greater labours, far more imprisonments, with countless beatings, and often near death'* (2Co 11:23–29).

Fourth, an Apostle must have steadfastly suffered persecution for Christ's sake. The Twelve, of course, from the very beginning had suffered persecution for preaching the word.

> And as they were speaking to the people, the priests
> and the captain of the temple and the Sadducees
> came upon them, annoyed because they were
> teaching the people and proclaiming in Jesus the
> resurrection from the dead. And they arrested them
> and put them in custody until the morrow, for it was
> already evening (Ac 4:1–3).

> When they had called in the apostles, they beat them
> and charged them not to speak in the name of Jesus,
> and let them go. Then they left the presence of the
> council, rejoicing that they were counted worthy to
> suffer dishonour for the name (Ac 5:40–41).

St Paul was no stranger to persecution and suffering for the sake of the Gospel as he told the Corinthians:

> Five times I have received at the hands of the Jews
> the forty lashes less one. Three times I have been
> beaten with rods; once I was stoned. Three times I
> have been shipwrecked; a night and a day I have
> been adrift at sea; on frequent journeys, in danger
> from rivers, danger from robbers, danger from my
> own people, danger from Gentiles, danger in the
> city, danger in the wilderness, danger at sea, danger
> from false brethren; in toil and hardship, through
> many a sleepless night, in hunger and thirst, often

without food, in cold and exposure. And, apart from other things, there is the daily pressure upon me of my anxiety for all the churches (2Co 11:24–28).

Figure 21: *St Paul is shipwrecked*

Fifth, an Apostle must prove himself by signs, wonders and mighty deeds: '*The signs of a true apostle were performed among you in all patience, with signs and wonders and mighty works'* (2Co 12:12).

Since the Apostles were ambassadors of Christ and held supreme authority in the Church, they could speak either on behalf of the Lord or by their own initiative. St Paul exercised his apostolic authority in various ways. For instance, he gave directives quoting the Lord's express command. Concerning the indissolubility of marriage, he stated: *'To the married I give charge, not I but the Lord, that the wife should not separate from her husband'* (1Co 7:10). He also gave directives on the right for preachers of the Gospel to live by the Gospel *'In the same way, the Lord commanded that those who proclaim the gospel should get their living by the gospel'* (1Co 9:14). Additionally, genuine prophets in the Church, he insisted, would recognise the divine inspiration of what he wrote, *'If anyone thinks that he is a prophet, or spiritual, he should acknowledge that what I am writing to you is a command of the Lord. If any one does not recognise this, he is not recognised'* (1Co 14:37–38).

Regarding the celibate and married state, he gave his own personal advice, which nevertheless was authoritative:

> I say this by way of concession, not of command (1Co 7:6) ... To the rest I say, not the Lord, that if any brother has a wife who is an unbeliever, and she consents to live with him, he should not divorce her. If any woman has a husband who is an unbeliever, and he consents to live with her, she should not divorce him (vv.12–14) ... Now concerning the unmarried, I have no command of the Lord, but I give my opinion as one who by the Lord's mercy is trustworthy (v. 25) ... But in my judgment she is happier if she remains as she is. And I think that I have the Spirit of God (v.40).

On a number of occasions, he exercised his apostolic right to command as when he gave instructions concerning the collections: *'Now concerning the contribution for the saints: as I directed the churches of Galatia, so you also are to do'* (1Co 16:1), or regarding divine worship:

> First of all, then, I urge that supplications, prayers, intercessions, and thanksgivings be made for all men, for kings and all who are in high positions, … God our Saviour, who desires all men to be saved and to come to the knowledge of the truth. (1Tm 2:1–4)

He also exercised his apostolic authority to regulate the use of the gifts of the Spirit:

> Let all things be done for edification. If any speak in a tongue, let there be only two or at most three, and each in turn; and let one interpret. But if there is no one to interpret, let each of them keep silence in church and speak to himself and to God. Let two or three prophets speak, and let the others weigh what is said. If a revelation is made to another sitting by, let the first be silent. For you can all prophesy one by one, so that all may learn and all be encouraged; and the spirits of prophets are subject to prophets (1Co 14:26–32).

He gave directions regarding the flesh offered to idols:

> Now concerning food offered to idols: we know that 'all of us possess knowledge.' 'Knowledge' puffs up, but love builds up … Hence, as to the eating of food offered to idols, we know that 'an idol has no real existence', and that 'there is no God but one' (1Co 8:1, 4).

The exercise of his apostolic authority is also seen in his promise to regulate matters in person: *'What do you wish? Shall I come to you with a rod, or with love in a spirit of gentleness?'* (1Co 4:21); and

> I beg of you that when I am present I may not have to show boldness with such confidence as I count on showing against some who suspect us of acting in worldly fashion. For though we live in the world we are not carrying on a worldly war (2Co 13:2–3).

On contentious issues, such as circumcision, he exercised his personal authority when he declared, *'Now I, Paul, say to you that if you receive circumcision, Christ will be of no advantage to you. I testify again to every man who receives circumcision that he is bound to keep the whole law'* (Ga 5:2–3). Although he argued with, entreated and coaxed the Galatians on the issue, he still expected to be obeyed because of his apostolic authority *'I have confidence in the Lord that you will take no other view than mine; and he who is troubling you will bear his judgment, whoever he is'* (Ga 5:10).

The Lord entrusted to His Church the power to forgive sins through the ministry of His Apostles. St Paul exercised this power when he forgave the sin of the incestuous Corinthian: *'Anyone whom you forgive, I also forgive. What I have forgiven, if I have forgiven anything, has been for your sake in the presence of Christ.'* (2Co 2:10)

St Peter

Christ entrusted to Simon Peter the office of leadership of the Church and of the apostolic College. In the Gospels, St Peter is the most prominent of the disciples and is mentioned no less than 176 times by name in the New Testament. After Christ's ascension into heaven, St Peter was the recognised and undisputed head of the Apostles, as can be seen in many of the incidents recorded in the Acts of the Apostles.

For instance, he took the lead and authoritatively addressed his ten co-Apostles, in the presence of Mary, the Mother of Jesus:

> and when they had entered, they went up to the upper room, where they were staying, Peter and John and James and Andrew, Philip and Thomas, Bartholomew and Matthew, James the son of Alphaeus and Simon the Zealot and Judas the son of James. All these with one accord devoted themselves to prayer, together with the women and Mary the mother of Jesus, and with his brothers (Ac 1:13–14).

Then, presiding over the company and interpreting the prophecy of Psalms 65:25 and 109:8, he called for a vote to be taken on who should replace Judas Iscariot:

For it is written in the book of Psalms, 'Let his habitation become desolate, and let there be no one to live in it'; and 'His office let another take.' So one of the men who has accompanied us during all the time that the Lord Jesus went in and out among us, beginning from the baptism of John until the day when he was taken up from us—one of these men must become with us a witness to his resurrection (Ac 1:20–22).

As leader of the Apostles and head of the Church, he preached to the crowds on the day of Pentecost. *'But Peter, standing with the eleven, lifted up his voice and addressed them, "Men of Judea and all who dwell in Jerusalem, let this be known to you, and give ear to my words"'* (Ac 2:14),and he received three thousand converts into Church: *'So those who received his word were baptized, and there were added that day about three thousand souls'* (Ac 2:41).

Figure 22: *An angel frees St Peter from prison*

He authoritatively received Cornelius and his household, the first Gentiles to be converted, into the Church. Cornelius was a devout and God–fearing Roman centurion and, during prayer, was instructed by an angel to send for Simon Peter (Ac 10:1–2), who apprised him of the life, death and Resurrection of Christ.

> While Peter was still saying this, the Holy Spirit fell on all who heard the word. And the believers from among the circumcised who came with Peter were amazed, because the gift of the Holy Spirit had been poured out even on the Gentiles. For they heard them speaking in tongues and extolling God. Then Peter declared, 'Can anyone forbid water for baptizing these people who have received the Holy Spirit just as we have?' And he commanded them to be baptized in the name of Jesus Christ (Ac 10:44–48).

The circumcision party within the Church in Jerusalem was initially critical of Peter's association with the Gentiles (Ac 11:2–3) but, once he had given an account of the events that led him to baptise Cornelius and his household, all criticism ceased. *'When they heard this they were silenced. And they glorified God, saying, "Then to the Gentiles also God has granted repentance unto life"'* (Ac 11:18).

Points to Remember

a. *The Apostles were the official witnesses to the life, death and Resurrection of Jesus Christ.*

b. *Christ commissioned them to teach all nations and He gave them authority to speak in His name and to act on His behalf.*

c. *With Simon Peter as head, the Apostles formed a Council or College that governed the Church Christ founded.*

d. *A true Apostle must be a Jew, must have seen Christ, must be a servant of Christ, must have suffered persecution for Christ's sake, and must prove himself by signs, wonders and might works.*

e. *By ordaining men who would succeed them in the governance of the Church, the Apostles established the apostolic succession. The successors of the Apostles are the bishops of the Church Christ founded.*

f. *Since the Apostolic Church was one, holy and catholic, apostolicity is the most important of the four characteristics of the Church Christ founded.*

11

Conclusion: Where is the Church Christ founded?

It has been shown using the Sacred Scriptures that Christ established a divine or supernatural society, called the Church, when He gave His Apostles the power to teach (Mt 28:19; Mk 16:15), to govern (Mt 18:18; Jn 20:21) and to sanctify (Mt 28:20; Jn 20:22; Lk 22:19) those who believe in Him. A true follower of Christ, then, will accept the Apostles' teaching (Mk 16:16), obey their decrees (Lk 10:16; Mt 18:17), and use the divinely instituted means of sanctification (Jn 3:5; 6:54), called sacraments.

A divine and human society

The Church, as a society, is divine in its origin and supernatural in its end and its means. It is, therefore, unfailing and perpetual, always opposed to the world as was Christ, her divine Founder, and always conquering her enemies, as Christ once won the victory of the resurrection through the seeming failure of the cross.

Despite its divine origin, the Church is, at the same time, a natural or human society because its members are human beings. This is why the Church is afflicted by scandals, heresies and schisms. Christ Himself foretold this would happen when, calling the Church the Kingdom of God, He described it as a field in which weeds grew together with the wheat, and as a net containing fish, good and bad alike (Mt 13:24, 47).

The Church Christ founded is endowed with specific characteristics that she might be recognised by all to whom the Lord has given '*a mind to understand or eyes to see or ears to hear*' (Dt 29:4; Ezk 12:2)as the Guardian and Teacher of the revealed word.

A visible society

The New Testament frequently represents the Church Christ founded as an external, visible society, which is called the house of God (1Tm 2:15), a kingdom (Mt 4:23; 13:24), a field (Mt 13:24), a grain of mustard seed that becomes a tree (Mt 13:31), a city set on a hill (Mt 5:14), a sheepfold (Jn 10:16) or a flock (Ac 20:28). If this Church were not an easily recognisable and visible society, Christ could not require anyone to believe under the penalty of damnation (Mk 16:18); nor could He direct that the Christian disobedient to the Church's commands be treated as '*a heathen and a publican*' (Mt 18:17).

St Paul plainly asserted that the Church Christ founded is visible to the faithful, as well as to unbelievers. It is visible to the faithful so that they may know whom to believe and whom to obey. (Rm 2:8) It is visible to unbelievers outside the fold so that they may accept with certainty the divinely accredited ambassadors of the Gospel of peace (Rm 10:14–15).

Throughout the New Testament, the Church Christ founded is spoken of as a divine, infallible teaching authority. Christ said that His Church is as a city built upon a rock foundation, which can never be destroyed by Satan and the powers of evil (Mt 16:18; cf. Mt 7:24; Ps 116:5).

With Himself as the cornerstone, Christ built His Church on the foundation of the Apostles (Ep 2:20; Rev 21:4) and entrusted the primacy to Simon Peter. As leader of the Apostles and visible head of the Church, Peter was to teach, govern and strengthen the flock of Christ (Jn 21:15–17; Lk 22:32) and his office was to endure until Christ's return at the end of time.

Founded on Peter and the Apostles

Throughout the Gospels, the mission of the apostles is declared as being identical with the mission of Christ and His heavenly Father, namely, to give infallible witness to the truth (Jn 18:37, cf. Mt 1:38, Jn 20:21, Jn 13:20; Mt 10:40; cf. Lk 10:16; Jn 12:44–48; Jn 15:20, 24). Since the Apostles were personally subject to death (Lk 21:16) and their mission was to last until Christ's return at the end of time, it follows that they were to have successors and they provided for this with the ordination of suitable men (1Tm 4:14; 5:22). This constitutes the apostolic succession and ensures the continuity and authenticity of the Church's mission.

Equally important to the Church's mission is the succession to Peter's office both as visible head of the Church and leader (Jn 21:3) of the Apostles. First, the Church, like every human society, needs a visible head and leader and second, Christ had entrusted to Simon Peter the specific mission and office of teaching, governing and strengthening the Church (Jn 21:15–17; Lk 22:32), His Mystical Body. Since the mission of the Church was to continue throughout the ages until Christ's return, she would need the benefits of Peter's mission and office, which could only be fulfilled when, upon the death of Simon Peter, a successor was chosen.

When Christ gave the Apostles the divine commission to teach all nations until the end of the time (Mt 28:20), He promised them His abiding presence '*I am with you always*', as well as the assistance of the Spirit of Truth, as a guarantee of the success of their mission to all nations throughout the ages until His second coming.

The Apostles always declared their teaching to be the word of God (Ac 4:31; 8:14; 12:24; 13:44; 15:35; 1Co 14:35; 2Tm 2:9), which they proclaimed infallibly by the assistance of the Holy Spirit (Ac 2:4; 4:31; 15:25–28; 1Co 2:4–16), who confirmed their witness by miracles (Ac 3:16; 4:29–31; 5:12, 16; 9:32–42). All contrary teaching is false and blasphemous, even if it were to come from an angel of God (Ac 13:18; Ga 1:8–9).

An indefectible Church

Christ established an indefectible Church (Mt 16:18), that is, a Church that would preserve its essential characteristics unimpaired in every age. If the Church had or were to suffer substantial change, it would no longer be capable of accomplishing the work for which Christ established it, and the '*gates of hell*' would have or could prevailed against it. Thus, if she could set up a false and corrupt moral standard, then she would not lead her members to holiness. If she could err in the slightest point of doctrine, she would not be speaking with the voice of Christ who is the Truth and who said, '*those who hear you, hear me.*' If she could err in the slightest, God would not require belief in her teaching and message under pain of eternal damnation. If she could lose her hierarchy and the sacraments, she would no longer be able to dispense the graces flowing from the Passion of her Founder to her members.

The Church Christ founded

From the foregoing discussion, it will now be easy to identify the Church Christ founded from among the innu-merable claimants of that distinction. Now since Christ founded only one Church, it is evident that only one of the claimants is truly that Church. The true Church has had to defend herself from apostolic times against the claims of dissident groups, presenting a deformed, corrupted, or perverted version of the Gospel. Today, since the claimants are so numerous, thirty thousand being a conservative estimate, it is not feasible to examine each individually. Therefore, the following approach will be used to identify the Church Christ founded.

First, it should be noted that it is possible to identify the founder of every church and the date of its beginning. Second, only the true Church will be able to trace her origin directly to Our Lord Jesus Christ and His Apostles. These two premises combine to establish the principle that the Church Christ founded must be able to trace her origin, doctrine and episcopal succession right back to Christ and His Apostles. Any church founded after apostolic times, therefore, cannot be the true Church, that is, the Church Christ founded.

Armed with the foregoing principle, it is clear that, since the Catholic Church alone possesses all four characteristics identified as belonging to the Church Christ founded, the Church Christ founded subsists in the Catholic Church. That is, the fullness of the Church Christ founded is to be found in the Catholic Church alone.

In His Sermon on the Mount, Christ extended a loving and encouraging invitation to every human being: '*Ask, and it will be given you; seek, and you will find; knock, and it will be opened to you. For every one who asks receives, and he who seeks finds, and to him who knocks it will be opened*' (Mt 7:7–8).

Figure 23: *The New Jerusalem*

All those, therefore, who wish to be true disciples of Christ must, like Andrew, ask Him 'Lord, where is your Church?' (Jn 1:38) Then, after a prayerful and honest search, they will arrive, by the light of the Holy Spirit, at the door of the Church Christ founded. Upon knocking on that door, Christ, just as He promised, will open the door to those seeking Him with a sincere heart; and, upon opening, He will welcome them into the joys of eternal life.

12

Epilogue: Christ founded the Catholic Church

Bishops

Christ founded one Church with the twelve Apostles forming its governing council and this included Simon Peter as its visible head. The Apostles, by ordaining men to succeed them and to carry on their mission, established the Church's apostolic succession. These men were called bishops and, as successors to the Apostles, formed the governing council of the Church over which the Pope, the bishop of Rome, himself a successor to Simon Peter, holds primacy. It is a historical fact that St Peter was in Rome and was martyred there in AD 67. He, himself, in his first Epistle, witnessed to his presence in Rome by stating that he was writing from Babylon, a code word for Rome in apostolic times (1P 5:13). Further, there are many testimonies from the first four centuries that St Peter was the first bishop of Rome and, no city, except Rome, has ever claimed to be the place of his death.

There are also historical documents in existence that name the leaders or bishops who governed the Church after the death of the Apostles and, in some cases, the actual writings of a number of these bishops, several of whom are called 'Fathers of the Church' still exist. The bishops, like the Apostles before them, had to confront both the teachers of false doctrine and the rebels against their authority. They did so by teaching the apostolic faith, which they had received and, by defining infallibly those things that placed a person outside the pale of the Church Christ founded. Such persons fall into one of two possible categories: the schismatic who reject the Church's authority and the heretical that reject both the Church's authority and teaching.

The Catholic Church

It is clear that the expression 'Catholic Church' is not explicitly found in the Bible. However, both the concept and the model are undeniably contained in the Old, as well as the New Testament and, from the earliest times, have been used to describe the Church Christ founded. Further, it should be noted that no heretical or schismatic group, even in the early Church, ever called itself Catholic and, none of the eastern schismatic Churches that seceded from Rome between the fifth and eleventh centuries ever denied the Roman Pontificate of St Peter. It is clear that one cannot be held responsible for a situation not of one's making and so, the sin of separation from the Catholic Church cannot be attributed to individuals born into non–Catholic Churches or ecclesial communities. Nevertheless, everyone is obliged to search for the true Church, the pearl of great price. In general, it can be observed that the Orthodox Churches, since they profess the Catholic faith and have valid apostolic succession but are severed from fraternal union with the Bishop of Rome, are schismatic. On the other hand, Protestant ecclesial communities are deemed heretical essentially because they substitute personal faith for the Catholic faith and reject both apostolic succession and authority of the Bishop of Rome.

The Roman Catholic Church fits exactly the profile of the Church Christ founded.

Apostolic

First, historically, as the oldest of all the claimants, the Catholic Church (with the Pope, the bishop of Rome and successor to Simon Peter, and the College of bishops forming its governing body) can trace her hierarchical lineage back, in unbroken succession, to the Apostles and so, validly claims to be an apostolic Church. Apostolicity is the first and most necessary mark and, of itself, constitutes a complete guarantee that Christ, who set up only one Church, established her.

Catholic

Second, the Church has known herself to be Catholic from her origin as is evident from the Apostles' Creed and the writings of her first bishops, some of whom are called Fathers of the Church. Thus,

a. The expression *Catholic Church* is first found in the letters of St Ignatius of Antioch. Born in Syria around the year AD 50, St Ignatius died a martyr's death in Rome sometime between AD 98 and AD 117. He was St Peter's second successor as bishop to the See of Antioch and, together with St Polycarp, was a disciple of St John the Evangelist. He wrote the Smyrnaeans: *'Where the bishop is, there the people should be; just as where Christ Jesus is, there also is the Catholic Church.'*

b. St Polycarp (AD 69–155), a disciple of St John the Evangelist, was bishop of Smyrna and before his arrest and martyrdom, he prayed for *'the whole Catholic Church spread all over the world.'*

c. During the pontificate of Pope Anicetus (AD 155–166), St Hegesippus (d. AD 156) travelled to Rome through Corinth from the East where he lived. As he journeyed through the various provinces of the empire, he examined the teachings and traced the apostolic succession of their churches to ascertain their uniformity with Rome. He wrote,

> And the Church of the Corinthians remained in the true word until Primus was bishop in Corinth; I made their acquaintance in my journey to Rome, and remained with the Corinthians many days, in which we were refreshed with the true word. And when I was in Rome, I made a succession up to Pope Anicetus, whose deacon was Eleutherus. And in

each succession and in each city all is according to the ordinances of the law and the Prophets and the Lord.

d. The Ecumenical Council of Nicea (AD 325) declared *'Rome has always held the primacy'* and separation from Rome is separation from the Catholic Church.

e. St Athanasius, bishop of Alexandria (AD 296–373) wrote

> It will not be irrelevant to examine the ancient tradition and the doctrine and faith of the Catholic Church which, as we know, the Lord handed down, the apostles preached and the fathers preserved. For on this tradition the Church is founded, and if anyone abandons it, he cannot be a Christian nor have any right to the name.

f. St Cyril, bishop of Jerusalem (315–386) taught

> I believe in the One, Holy Catholic Church because she is spread all over the earth and because she universally and uninterruptedly teaches all the doctrines of faith necessary for a man to know; because she presses into God's service the whole human race, rulers or subjects, learned or unlearned; and lastly because she heals all maladies of soul and body.

He also wrote

> But since the word 'Church' is applied to different things (including the meeting places of heretics, the Marcionists, the Manichees and others) the Faith has given you by way of security, the article of the Creed: 'I believe in One, Holy, Catholic Church' so that you can avoid their wretched meetings and ever abide within the Holy Catholic Church in which you were reborn. And if you are ever passing through any city, don't just ask where is the Lord's House, but where is the Catholic Church. For this is the special name of this holy body, the Mother of us all, the Spouse of our Lord Jesus Christ, the only–begotten Son of God.

g. St Pacianus, bishop of Barcelona in Spain wrote in AD 365 '*My first name is Christian, my surname is Catholic*'.

h. St Augustine (AD 354–430), bishop of Hippo, in his controversy with the schismatic Donatists called himself a Catholic Christian and wrote, '*The Church is diffused by the splendour of one faith from the rising to the setting sun.*'

He also told them

> Whoever is separated from this Catholic Church, however innocently he thinks he lives, for this fault alone that he separated from the unity of Christ, will not have life; the anger of God remains on him.

St Augustine further stated

> All the Assemblies or rather divisions that call themselves Churches of Christ but which in fact have separated themselves from the unity of the Church, do not belong to the true Church. They might indeed belong to her if the Holy Spirit could be divided against himself, but as this is impossible, they do not belong to her.

i. St Vincent of Lerins (d. AD 435) defined as Catholic those things that are believed '*always, everywhere and by everybody*' —'*quod semper, ubique et ab omnibus.*' That is, catholicity implies antiquity, universality and consent.

Throughout history, all sects initially draw their members from among Catholics whom they either seduce, coerced or enticed rather from among non–Christian peoples. Thus, according to Tertullian (AD 160–220)

> They make it their business not to convert the heathen, but to subvert our people. This is rather the glory, which they seek: to bring about the fall of those who stand—not to raise up those who have fallen. Accordingly, since the very work they propose comes not from the building up of their own society but from demolishing the truth, they undermine our edifices, so that they can construct their own.

According to St Augustine, there were more than 90 different heresies in the first 400 years of the Church's existence. It is a historical fact, however, that while individual sects may die out, their heretical ideas frequently resurface centuries later, as they did, for example, in the sixteenth century and do even today. Between 1517 and 1600, the rebellion against Church teaching and authority, instigated by Martin Luther, (1483–1546) generated over 270 different Protestant sects, holding different principles with no central authoritative teaching. Founded on the false principle of private interpretation of Scripture (2P 1:20–21; 3:15–16), they have multiplied exponentially, so that today there are over 38,000 different faith bodies, each claiming to be, or to be a part of, the authentic Church Christ founded (See Appendix 1).

The schism of the Orthodox Churches in AD 1054 reduced them to national and cultural churches. As a result, they lost their catholicity as is evidenced in the fact they have undertaken very little in the way of missionary work. The missionary activity of the Catholic Church, however, has always been directed to those who are not baptised but Protestant sects today, as the heretics of old, recruit their numbers from the ranks of Catholic and Orthodox Christians, boasting of the numbers of Catholics in Latin America, the Philippines and Asia who have converted to their version of Christianity (Ga 1:7–8).

Only one religious body fulfils Christ's command to make disciples of all nations (Mt 28:19–20) and which can therefore claim to be authentically catholic. The Church, which owns the Bishop of Rome as its supreme head extends its ministrations over the whole world, thus fulfilling its obligation to preach the Gospel to all peoples. The Orthodox Churches are even today, only national, regional or cultural churches in local schism. Although there were radical independent sects among them, the older Protestant communities were initially national or cultural entities under the control of the State. The more recent ones, founded mostly in nineteenth-century America, are less so and, initially none of them ever attempted to establish a universal mission. For nearly three hundred years after Martin Luther's rebellion, a universal missionary enterprise was unknown among Protestant bodies. In the nineteenth century, it is true, some of them attempted the conversion of non-Christian peoples and contributed large sums of money for this purpose but even so, this was done within restricted areas, as in the case of the Anglicans, a linguistic and so not a universal communion, that evangelised only within the confines of the British Empire. The means of rapid communication and ease of travel in the modern world has now made a universal mission possible for most sects. The lack, however, of a central authoritative voice results in the appearance of more and more factions, estimated at five new ones each day.

One

Third, the Catholic Church is one. Her oneness follows from her catholicity since those who reject her authority or deny her doctrine separate themselves from her unity just as dead branches detached from the vine. Most institutions can maintain a form of unity for a period of time within some narrow area; the Catholic Church's unity, however, not only covers two millennia but also extends over the entire face of the earth.

Holy

Fourth, the Catholic Church is holy. Holiness implies nearness to God, the author and source of all holiness. (Is 6:3; Rev 4:8) For this reason, the Bible refers to certain places as holy because God has specially blessed them (Ex 3:5; Mt 4:5); to certain things as holy because they have been dedicated to divine worship (Ex 29:29; Heb 9:2); and to certain persons as holy because they are closely united to God by charity. (Tb 2:12; Rm 1:7; Rev 5:3)

The Church receives her holiness from God

The Catholic Church is holy because her Founder and Head, Jesus Christ, is God, the infinite source of all holiness. As man, He alone could confidently challenge His enemies: *'Which of you can convict Me of sin?'* (Jn 8:46; Lk 1:35) Her holiness emanates from the Spirit who dwells within and because of the graces that He bestows on her, she has produced members, distinguished by pre–eminent holiness, that is, by their closeness to God. The Catholic Church claims the apostolic authority to recognise and to declare the heroic sanctity of her members who are called saints. No Protestant body claims this authority or power inherently, and generally, they all implicitly refute it.

The Church leads her members to holiness

The Catholic Church is holy because of her intimate union with Christ, as His Bride (Ep 5:23–32) and His Mystical Body. (1Co 12:27; Ep 1:22; 4:11; 5:30) Catholics are the *'chosen people'* and a *'holy nation'* because they are branches of the true Vine, Christ Jesus. (Jn 15:5)Since God desires the salvation of all, it is possible that those who, through invincible ignorance, are outside her visible fold may, in fact, be her members by desire. If such were indeed the case, then they would share in her divine life through elements of sanctification and truth derived from the fullness of grace and truth that Christ (Jn 15:1–6) entrusted to His Church.

The Catholic Church is holy, not because there are no sinners within her fold (Mt 13:24–30; 47–48) but, because her one aim is to produce holiness (Ep 5:25–27) in her children. The ideal she presents to the world is identical with that which Christ presented. (Mt 5:48) She has always preserved uncorrupted the entire Gospel of Christ for she wants her children to possess the same mind that is in Christ Jesus. (Phil.2:5) She has always faithfully interpreted the commandments and the counsels of Christ, the Saviour, who not only reinforced but also spiritualised the Ten

Commandments (Mt 5:17–47) and invited His followers to seek perfection. (Mt 5:48; 19:21) She has always infallibly given her children the means of grace instituted by Christ Himself in the Sacrifice of the Mass, and in the seven sacraments. Though not everyone will readily accept this teaching, these are the ordinary means by which the precious Blood of Christ, shed upon the cross, is applied today to individuals for their sanctification and redemption. (Mt 19:11–12)

Members of the Church

Christ came to call not the virtuous but sinners to repentance (Mt 9:13; Mk 2:17; Lk 5:32). Hence, His Church, the Catholic Church, cannot be a Church of the elect or of the sinless; nor can it be an exclusive club of the outwardly respectable and the well-to-do. Christ's Church is not a hotel for saints but a hospital for sinners. Even though the Church, because she has no other life but the life of grace, is holy, she is, nonetheless, on account of her sinful members always in need of purification. It follows then, that the virtues of individual Catholics are in direct proportion to their faithful acceptance of all the means of sanctification that the Church offers them. These means include the acceptance of her doctrines, the observance of her commandments and counsels, the faithful attendance at holy Mass and the frequent and fruitful reception of her Sacraments. Critics point scornfully at the Catholic Church whenever wayward members disobey her laws and neglect her sacraments. These, however, are Catholics who have strayed from Christ. They are not normative of those whose lives are in accordance with Catholic principles and, despite the gravity of their transgressions, they cannot impair the Church's inherent ability to sanctify her members. Furthermore, the accusations that the Church's critics level against her could only be valid if her teachings did indeed condone her transgressing members' sinful behaviour.

Moral teaching of the Church

Instead of directing disapproval at the deeds of the Church's transgressing members, many critics attempt to justify the unacceptable behaviour by levelling accusations against the Church's moral teaching, which those critics regarded as being either too high or unrealistic. The substance of the Church's moral doctrine was clearly established by Jesus Christ who declared that even a lustful look was adulterous (Mt 5:28). The Church, in inviting her members to imitate the life of Christ, encourages them in the practice of good works, of self-sacrifice, of love of suffering and, especially that of the three evangelical counsels of perfection, namely, voluntary poverty, perfect chastity and entire obedience. In this, the Church proposes to her members the divine ideal. The sects that have severed themselves from the Church have either neglected or repudiated some part of the Apostles' moral teaching in this regard. The Reformers of the sixteenth century went as far as denying the value of good works altogether. Although many contemporary Protestants have rejected their forebears' anti-Christian doctrine, they still regard the self-surrender in religious life by priests, monks and nuns as folly.

Sacraments of the Church

The Church, the Mystical Body of Christ, possesses the Holy Mass by which the sacrifice of Christ upon the cross is renewed everyday upon her altars. By Baptism, Catholics are united to Christ as the branch is united to the vine (Jn 15:1–6); and grace is infused into their souls so that they become *'partakers of the divine nature'* (2P 1:4). By the other sacraments, this personal union is strengthened, deepened and intensified. This is especially true in Holy Communion where a Catholic is most intimately joined to Christ, in fulfilment of His promise that those who eat His flesh and drink His blood would share His divine life (Jn 6:57).

Doctrine of the Church

Reason and revelation both demand that the Teacher of Christ's divine revelation speak as Christ did, infallibly. Thus, by divine guidance, the Catholic Church, as the Custodian and Teacher of divine revelation is kept free from teaching erroneous doctrine. This is logical for two reasons. First, since God is good and *'wishes everyone to be saved and come to the knowledge of the truth,'* (1Tm 2:4) it is unthinkable that He would fail to provide His revelation with a living infallible witness. Second, because God is just, He would not command His children to believe under penalty of hell (Mk 16:16) while, at the same time, leaving them to the tricks of every false prophet (Mt 13:21) and lying teacher (2P 2:1) preaching a Gospel contrary to His own. (Ga 1:8) While St Paul declared that *'All scripture is inspired by God and profitable for teaching, for reproof, for correction, and for training in righteousness'* (2Tm 3:16), he also made it abundantly clear that it is the Church, not the Scriptures that is the *'pillar and bulwark of truth'* (1Tm 3:15). Moreover, not only was the Church in existence and functioning for many years before the first line of the New Testament was written but, also, it was the Church that authoritatively and infallibly decided which writings were, in fact, inspired by God and therefore part of Sacred Scripture. It also follows from a definitive declaration of St Peter that only the Church Christ founded, that is, the Catholic Church, can authoritatively interpret the true meaning of any passage of Scripture: *'First of all you must understand this, that no prophecy of scripture is a matter of one's own interpretation, because no prophecy ever came by the impulse of man, but men moved by the Holy Spirit spoke from God'* (2P 1:20–21).

Christ and His Church

Christ, who is King, Prophet and Priest, revealed His triple office by declaring Himself to be the Way, the Truth and the Life. (Jn 14:5) It follows then, that as King, He governs the conduct of the faithful, as Prophet He reveals the life–giving truths they are to believe and as Priest He offers Himself, on behalf of sinners, to the Father as the Lamb who takes away the sin of the world. (Jn 1:29) Since the Catholic Church is Christ's Mystical Body, she alone represents Christ, the divine, infallible Teacher in conduct, in belief and in worship. The Church shares Christ's triple office of Priest, Prophet and King. She partakes in His priestly office when, at the holy Sacrifice of the Mass, she offers the eternal Victim to the heavenly Father for the redemption of the world. When proclaiming the eternal liberating Truth that makes believers free, she exercises Christ's prophetic mission. The Church participates in Christ's kingly government when, in passing moral judgments about conduct, she directs the faithful along the path of life.

In his book *Against Heresies*, St Ireneaus of Lyon wrote in AD 180 that

> the tradition derived from the apostles, of the very great, the very ancient, and universally known Church founded and organised at Rome by the two most glorious apostles, Peter and Paul, ... which comes down to our time by means of the successions of the bishops ... is a pre–eminent authority, ... For it is a matter of necessity that every Church should agree with this Church, on account of its pre–eminent authority, ... inasmuch as the tradition has been preserved continuously by those [faithful men] who exist everywhere' (Book III, Chapter 3, Para. 2).

Included in this same book, are the names of all the successors of St Peter, the first Bishop of Rome, up to the end of the second century. Appendix 2 offers a complete list of St Peter's successors, an unbroken, uninterrupted papal succession.

'*Great indeed, we confess, is the mystery of our religion*' (1Tm 3:16) that '*Christ Jesus, who, though he was in the form of God, did not count equality with God a thing to be grasped, but emptied himself, taking the form of a servant, being born in the likeness of men. And being found in human form he humbled himself and became obedient unto death, even death on a cross*' (Ph 2:5–8) and that, even though

He has withdrawn His visible presence, He remains, until the end of the time, with His Church and that this Church is none other than the Catholic Church, with the Bishop of Rome, the successor of Blessed Peter, as her visible head on earth.

APPENDIX 1

Christianity can be grouped into three broad categories. There is first the Catholic Church founded by Christ with her consistent, unchanging doctrine, sacramental system and line of authority stretching back to the Lord Jesus Himself.

Although they are preceded by the Ancient Churches of the East who, because of theological disputes, broke away at various times during the first millennium, the second category consists principally of the Orthodox Churches who separated in AD 1054 due to conflicts over papal authority. For the most part, they retain the Catholic Faith, Apostolic Succession and the sacramental system.

The Protestant revolution of the Sixteenth Century rejected the doctrine and authority of the Catholic Church and asserted the Bible alone (*Sola Scriptura*) as the only rule of faith and with it the claim that one can interpret the Bible for oneself. With no universal governing authority, the Protestant principle resulted not only in the establishing of national churches (Lutheran and Anglican) but also produced a myriad of radical sects inspired by the theology of John Calvin and others. Delving into the Bible, some groups attempted to recover the Apostolic Church, but the result was only more breaks with a further mushrooming of sects. The overall result is a conservative estimate of there being 38,000 different Protestant denomination and sects. Thus, in the nearly 500 years since Martin Luther's break with Rome, this number averages to at least one new Protestant denomination or sect developing every week.

Founders of some Christian denominations

Year AD	Founder	Denomination	Place
33	OUR LORD JESUS CHRIST	CATHOLIC CHURCH, founded with Simon Peter as its visible head	Palestine
431	Nestorius	Churches of the East	Constantinople
451	Eutyches	Oriental Orthodox Churches	Alexandria, Egypt
1054	Michael Cerularius	Eastern Orthodox Churches	Byzantium
1177	Peter Waldo	Waldensians	Lyons, France
1517	Martin Luther	Lutherans	Germany
1519	Huldrych Zwingli	Anabaptists	Switzerland
1534	Henry VIII	Church of England, Anglicans	England
1536	John Calvin	Calvinism; Dutch Reformed	Switzerland
1540	Menno Simons	Mennonites	Friesland
1560	John Knox	Presbyterians	Scotland
1570	Thomas Cartwright	Puritans	England
1582	Robert Browne	Congregationalists	England
1605	John Smith	Baptists	Holland
1654	George Fox	Society of Friends (Quakers)	England
1672	Stephen Mumford	Seventh Day Baptists	USA
1693	Jakob Ammann	Amish	Switzerland
1744	John & Charles Wesley	Methodists	England
1784	Samuel Seabury	Episcopalians	USA

Year AD	Founder	Denomination	Place
1800	Alexander Campbell and Barton Stone	Churches of Christ, Disciples of Christ	USA
1846	William Miller	Adventists	USA
1863	Ellen G. White	Seventh Day Adventists	USA
1865	William and Catherine Booth	Salvation Army	England
1867	From Methodism	Holiness churches	USA
1900	Charles Parham	Pentecostals	USA
1908	Phineas F. Bresee	Church of the Nazarene	USA
1914	From Pentecostalism	Assemblies of God	USA
1955	Jim Jones	People's Temple	USA
1993	David Koresh	Branch Davidians	Waco, USA

Founders of some sects

Year AD	Founder	Sect	Place
1774	Theophilus Lindsey	Unitarians	England
1830	Joseph Smith	Mormons (Latter day saints)	USA
1848	John Thomas	Christadelphians	USA
1876	Charles T. Russell	Jehovah's Witnesses	USA
1879	Mary Baker Eddy	Christian Science	USA
1934	Herbert W. Armstrong	Worldwide Church of God	USA
1953	L. Ron Hubbard	Church of Scientology	USA
1954	Sun Myung Moon	Moonies	Korea

The Protestant movement of the sixteenth-century originated from four sources: Martin Luther, John Calvin, Huldrych Zwingli and Henry VIII. Founded on the premise that each person can interpret Scripture for himself, they soon fractured into innumerable factions, each with its own peculiar version of the Christian faith. In broad strokes, these are some of the offshoots of the original four sixteenth-century reform movements.

Luther: *Lutherans, Pietists, Moravians, Baptist General Conference, Free Churches.*

Calvin: *Presbyterians, Universalism, Christian Reformed, Dutch Reformed, Huguenots, Evangelicals, Puritans, Congregational, Quakers, Shakers, Adventists.*

Zwingli: *Anabaptists, Hutterites, Mennonites, Baptists, Brethren, Separatists, Congregationalists, Amish.*

Henry VIII: *Anglicans, Episcopalians, Methodists, Holiness churches, Assemblies of God, Pentecostalism.*

The Unitarians, Mormons, Christadelphians, Jehovah's Witnesses, Christian Scientists, Worldwide Church of God, Church of Scientology and the Moonies are not, in any way, Christian denominations but sects, since they do not profess belief in either the Trinity or the Incarnation of Christ; in short they do not believe that Christ is God. They are, however, included in this listing because their founders came from Christian backgrounds and sometimes they gain followers from that same background.

APPENDIX 2

Bishops of Rome: Popes

First and Second Centuries

1.   St Peter (42–67)
2.   St Linus (67–79)
3.   St Anacletus (79–92)
4.   St Clement I (92–101)
5.   St Evaristus (101–105)
6.   St Alexander I (105–115)
7.   St Sixtus I (115–125)
8.   St Telesphorus (125–136)
9.   St Hyginis (136–140)
10. St Pius I (140–155)
11. St Anicetus (155–166)
12. St Soter (166–175)
13. St Eleutherius (175–189)
14. St Victor I (189–199)
15. St Zephyrinus (199–217)

Third and Fourth Centuries

16. St Callistus I (217–222)
17. St Urban I (222–230)
18. St Pontian (230–235)
19. St Anterius (235–236)
20. St Fabian (236–250)
21. St Cornelius (251–253)
22. St Lucius I (253–254)
23. St Stephen I (254–257)
24. St Sixtus II (257–258)
25. St Dionysius (259–268)
26. St Felix I (269–274)
27. St Eutychian (275–283)
28. St Gaius/Caius (283–296)
29. St Marcellinus (296–304)

30. St Marcellus I (308–309)
31. St Eusebius (309)
32. St Miltiades (311–314)
33. St Sylvester I (314–335)
34. St Mark (336)
35. St Julius I (337–352)
36. Liberius (352–366)
37. St Damasus I (366–384)
38. St Siricius (384–399)
39. St Anastasius I (399–401)

Fifth and Sixth Centuries

40. St Innocent I (401–417)
41. St Zosimus (417–418)
42. St Boniface I (418–422)
43. St Celestine I (422–432)
44. St Sixtus III (432–440)
45. St Leo I (440–461)
46. St Hilary (461–468)
47. St Simplicius (468–483)
48. St Felix III/II (483–492)
49. St Gelasius I (492–496)
50. Anastasius II (496–498)
51. St Symmachus (498–514)
52. St Hormisdas (514–523)
53. St John I (523–526)
54. St Felix IV/III (526–530)
55. Boniface II (530–532)
56. John II (533–535)
57. St Agapitus I (535–536)
58. St Silverius (536–537)
59. Vigilius (537–555)
60. Pelagius I (556–561)
61. John III (561–574)
62. Benedict I (575–579)
63. Pelagius II (579–590)
64. St Gregory I (590–604)

Seventh and Eighth Centuries

65.	Sabinian (604–606)
66.	Boniface III (607)
67.	St Boniface IV (608–615)
68.	St Deusdedit I (615–618)
69.	Boniface V (619–625)
70.	Honorius I (625–638)
71.	Severinus (640)
72.	John IV (640–642)
73.	Theodore I (642–649)
74.	St Martin I (649–655)
75.	St Eugene I (654–657)
76.	St Vitalian (657–672)
77.	Deusdedit II (672–676)
78.	Donus (676–678)
79.	St Agatho (678–681)
80.	St Leo II (682–683)
81.	St Benedict II (684–685)
82.	John V (685–686)
83.	Conon (686–687)
84.	St Sergius I (687–701)
85.	John VI (701–705)
86.	John VII (705–707)
87.	Sisinnius (708)
88.	Constantine (708–715)
89.	St Gregory II (715–731)
90.	St Gregory III (731–741)
91.	St Zachary (741–752)
92.	Stephen (II) (752)
93.	Stephen II/III (752–757)
94.	St Paul I (757–767)
95.	Stephen III/IV (768–772)
96.	Adrian I (772–795)
97.	St Leo III (795–816)

Ninth and Tenth Centuries

98.	Stephen IV/V (816–817)
99.	St Paschal I (817–824)
100.	Eugene II (824–827)
101.	Valentine (827)
102.	Gregory IV (827–844)
103.	Sergius II (844–847)
104.	St Leo IV (847–855)
105.	Benedict III (855–858)
106.	St Nicholas I (858–867)
107.	Adrian II (867–872)
108.	John VIII (872–882)
109.	Marinus I (882–884)
110.	St Adrian III (884–885)
111.	St Stephen V/VI (885–891)
112.	Formosus (891–896)
113.	Boniface VI (896)
114.	Stephen VI/VII (896–897)
115.	Romanus (897)
116.	Theodore II (897)
117.	John IX (898–900)
118.	Benedict IV (900–903)
119.	Leo V (903)
120.	Sergius III (904–911)
121.	Anastasius III (911–913)
122.	Lando (913–914)
123.	John X (914–928)
124.	Leo VI (928)
125.	Stephen VII/VIII (928–931)
126.	John XI (931–935)
127.	Leo VII (936–939)
128.	Stephen VIII/IX (939–942)
129.	Marinus II (942–946)
130.	Agapitus II (946–955)
131.	John XII (955–964)
132.	Leo VIII (963–965)
133.	Benedict V (964–966)

134.	John XIII (965–972)
135.	Benedict VI (973–974)
136.	Benedict VII (974–983)
137.	John XIV (983–984)
138.	John XV (984–996)
139.	Gregory V (996–999)
140.	Silvester II (999–1003)

Eleventh and Twelfth Centuries

141.	John XVII (1003)
142.	John XVIII (1004–1009)
143.	Sergius IV (1009–1012)
144.	Benedict VIII (1012–1024)
145.	John XIX (1024–1032)
146.	Benedict IX (1) (1032–1044)
147.	Silvester III (1045)
148.	Benedict IX (2) (1045)
149.	Gregory VI (1045–1046)
150.	Clement II (1046–1047)
151.	Benedict IX (3) (1047–1048)
152.	Damasus II (1048)
153.	St Leo IX (1049–1054)
154.	Victor II (1055–1057)
155.	Stephen IX/X (1057–1058)
156.	Nicholas II (1059–1061)
157.	Alexander II (1061–1073)
158.	St Gregory VII (1073–1085)
159.	Bl Victor III (1086–1087)
160.	Bl Urban II (1088–1099)
161.	Paschal II (1099–1118)
162.	Gelasius II (1118–1119)
163.	Callistus II (1119–1124)
164.	Honorius II (1124–1130)
165.	Innocent II (1130–1143)
166.	Celestine II (1143–1144)
167.	Lucius II (1144–1145)
168.	Bl Eugene III (1145–1153)

169. Anastasius IV (1153–1154)
170. Adrian IV (1154–1159)
171. Alexander III (1159–1181)
172. Lucius III (1181–1185)
173. Urban III (1185–1187)
174. Gregory VIII (1187)
175. Clement III (1187–1191)
176. Celestine III (1191–1198)
177. Innocent III (1198–1216)

Thirteenth and Fourteenth Centuries

178. Honorius III (1216–1227)
179. Gregory IX (1227–1241)
180. Celestine IV (1241)
181. Innocent IV (1243–1254)
182. Alexander IV (1254–1261)
183. Urban IV (1261–1264)
184. Clement IV (1265–1268)
185. Bl Gregory X (1271–1276)
186. Bl Innocent V (1276)
187. Adrian V (1276)
188. John XXI (1276–1277)
189. Nicholas III (1277–1280)
190. Martin IV (1281–1285)
191. Honorius IV (1285–1287)
192. Nicholas IV (1288–1292)
193. St Celestine V (1292)
194. Boniface VIII (1292–1303)
195. Bl. Benedict XI (1303–1304)
196. Clement V (1305–1314)
197. John XXII (1316–1334)
198. Benedict XII (1334–1342)
199. Clement VI (1342–1352)
200. Innocent VI (1352–1362)
201. Bl Urban V (1362–1370)
202. Gregory XI (1370–1378)
203. Urban VI (1378–1389)

204.   Boniface XI (1389–1404)

Fifteenth and Sixteenth Centuries

205.   Innocent VII (1404–1406)
206.   Gregory XII (1406–1415)
207.   Martin V (1417–1431)
208.   Eugene IV (1431–1447)
209.   Nicholas V (1447–1455)
210.   Callistus III (1455–1458)
211.   Pius II (1458–1464)
212.   Paul II (1464–1471)
213.   Sixtus IV (1471–1484)
214.   Innocent VIII (1484–1492)
215.   Alexander VI (1492–1503)
216.   Pius III (1503)
217.   Julius II (1503–1513)
218.   Leo X (1513–1521)
219.   Adrian VI (1522–1523)
220.   Clement VII (1523–1534)
221.   Paul III (1534–1549)
222.   Julius III (1550–1555)
223.   Marcellus II (1555)
224.   Paul IV (1555–1559)
225.   Pius IV (1559–1565)
226.   St Pius V (1566–1572)
227.   Gregory XIII (1572–1585)
228.   Sixtus V (1585–1590)
229.   Urban VII (1590)
230.   Gregory XIV (1590–1591)
231.   Innocent IX (1591)
232.   Clement VIII (1592–1605)

Seventeenth and Eighteenth Centuries

233.   Leo XI (1605)
234.   Paul V (1605–1621)
235.   Gregory XV (1621–1623)
236.   Urban VIII (1623–1644)

237.   Innocent X (1644–1655)
238.   Alexander VII (1655–1667)
239.   Clement IX (1667–1669)
240.   Clement X (1670–1676)
241.   Bl Innocent XI (1676–1689)
242.   Alexander VIII (1689–1691)
243.   Innocent XII (1691–1700)
244.   Clement XI (1700–1721)
245.   Innocent XIII (1721–1724)
246.   Benedict XIII (1724–1730)
247.   Clement XII (1730–1740)
248.   Benedict XIV (1740–1758)
249.   Clement XIII (1758–1769)
250.   Clement XIV (1769–1774)
251.   Pius VI (1775–1799)

Nineteenth, Twentieth and Twenty–First Centuries

252.   Pius VII (1800–1823)
253.   Leo XII (1823–1829)
254.   Pius VIII (1829–1830)
255.   Gregory XVI (1831–1846)
256.   Bl Pius IX (1846–1878)
257.   Leo XIII (1878–1903)
258.   St Pius X (1903–1914)
259.   Benedict XV (1914–1922)
260.   Pius XI (1922–1939)
261.   Pius XII (1939–1958)
262.   Bl John XXIII (1958–1963)
263.   Paul VI (1963–1978)
264.   John Paul I (1978)
265.   Bl John Paul II (1978–2005)
266.   Benedict XVI (2005–

Based on material in *The Annuario Pontificio*, Vatican City.